If Nuns Were Wives

If Nuns Were Wives

A Handbook on Marriage
from the Perspective of a Nun

SHANI CHEN

NEW YORK

NASHVILLE • MELBOURNE • VANCOUVER

If Nuns Were Wives

A Handbook on Marriage from the Perspective of a Nun

Published in New York, New York, by Morgan James Publishing. Morgan James is a trademark of Morgan James, LLC. www.MorganJamesPublishing.com

The Morgan James Speakers Group can bring authors to your live event. For more information or to book an event visit The Morgan James Speakers Group at www.TheMorganJamesSpeakersGroup.com.

ISBN 9781683505532 paperback
ISBN 9781683505549 eBook
Library of Congress Control Number: 2017906373

Interior Design by:
Chris Treccani
www.3dogdesign.net

In an effort to support local communities, raise awareness and funds, Morgan James Publishing donates a percentage of all book sales for the life of each book to Habitat for Humanity Peninsula and Greater Williamsburg.

Get involved today! Visit
www.MorganJamesBuilds.com

For my teachers who taught me to live with compassion.

CONTENTS

FOREWORD

Kristine Carlson

If Nuns Were Wives offers unique lessons and values forged through the life experiences of a well-trained spiritual woman whose dream of becoming a servant to humanity was initially shattered but later rediscovered through her role as wife and mother.

Marriage is not the easiest of institutions. It requires mindfulness, heart, compassion, unconditional acceptance and often the kind of wisdom that comes with true maturity. It also requires something even bigger and more spiritual than what most people have to offer their mate—*reverence*.

This book will teach you how to have the kind of pure heart where reverence can become the center of your relationship. In our closest relationships, we are but mirrors of one another and it takes tremendous devotion and commitment to build a partnership that stems from mutual respect and friendship. These things are paramount to what is required for a couple to flourish in marriage.

If Nuns Were Wives is full of gentle guidance through anecdotal stories that you will admire and relate to, leaving you with a feeling of "I can do it this way, too." Shani shows simple ways to practice the kind of internal mental dynamic and perspective one must possess in order to combat some of the demons that come when people sweat the small stuff in love.

On a day-to-day basis of living together, often in a smaller than adequate space, two people can bump up against each other—emotionally and physically—and become annoyed with each other. I like to think of this process in marriage as two stones polishing each other to what can become marital bliss. It is the relationship and internal dialogue you have with yourself that matters most. Shani shares with you the discipline and devotion it takes to overcome the obstacles that afflict your mind. Otherwise, those hindrances, if left unattended and untrained, can diminish that loving connection to your partner.

I know as you turn these pages, you will be captivated as I was by the wisdom and inspiration that come from a young woman's journey and her virtue. This is a book of virtue that will touch your heart as it did mine and help you become a woman of devotion, wisdom and deep connection to all that you hold dear. You will learn the art of reverence that, when given, is received in the fullness of what marriage offers you, your partner, and your family.

Thank you for sharing your heart, Shani.

Treasure the gifts of life and love,

Kris

PREFACE

I was in a temple kneeling before the altar, with my head dipped and my heart broken. My vision blurred with tears and reality swirled around me as I kneeled there weakly. It was the summer of 2007 in Kaohsiung, Taiwan. I had just been informed that I would not be accepted into the nunnery as a nun and that I'd have to return to my home in America. When I understood the meaning of those words, my spirit fell with despair. I didn't know what to do but to fall on my knees and sob. I was inconsolable.

For years, I had been preparing to enter the nunnery. For as long as I could remember, I had wanted to shave my head and don a robe. I dreamed of living with fellow sisters to practice spirituality and to become a vessel of purity. The simple life appealed to me very much and I longed to be tucked away somewhere to quietly practice religion for the rest of my days. I even gave away all my belongings and wrote goodbye letters to friends thinking I was destined to reside in the temple and to live a life of service to living beings.

But fate had different plans for me. Fate wanted me to practice spirituality in a different realm.

On September 27th, 2013, I married my husband in the court of Orange County, California. Instead of donning a robe, I donned a white dress. My practice of peace would soon begin outside the temple walls—far from it. But the pieces of my destiny would fall into place and become clear in due time.

I struggled in marriage initially. This came as a surprise to me because I thought that with my previous spiritual training, living with another person would come easily. But there were still many things to be worked through. It actually took a lot of discipline and diligence to achieve harmony in the home with my partner. I finally understood why so many marriages are unsuccessful despite them being such an alluring feature in life. It's because marriages usually don't stand a chance against afflictions. Each person is full of inner afflictions that lurk deep within the mind. When two people are made to live with one another in a small space, everything buried deep comes out—all the emotional baggage, all the hurts, pains, imperfections, violence, rage and insecurity that lie deep within each being. When disagreements arise, these monsters often surge out with fiery intensity. Contempt and hatred are easily bred in the home due to the lack of restraint humans possess towards these evils. As a result, an overwhelming number of marriage separations surface across nations around the globe.

Through the years, I've found that the only way to combat this enemy is to find a stronger opponent to counter the malice. The force must be more powerful than the strong afflictions that often overtake one's spirit. That is where my experience of wanting to become a nun comes into play. Nuns actively seek methods to purify their afflictions and to become beacons of light. They are soldiers of compassion and wisdom, seeking to reach perfection of the mind. Their rare and precious attitude allows them to thrive on difficulties while others in the world are squashed by them. Obstacles are fuel for the nuns' practice which only make them stronger. In this way, they hold the answers to finding peace and harmony in any situation including marriage.

To address a colossal problem, you need a colossal solution. And in this case, the nuns are finally worthy contenders for that which dissolves sacred unions. Those who are married could definitely benefit from the advice of experts who train twenty-four hours a day, seven days a week in virtue.

For nearly two decades, I walked in the footsteps of the nuns. Because of my aspiration to eventually join them, I diligently studied their ways and worked to emulate their behaviors. Through the years, I came to know their "software" very well.

After I became a wife, I realized that the software of a nun actually works in the hardware of a marriage! The things I had learned from the nuns helped me eventually succeed in an area that is difficult for so many.

My wish now is to share what I've learned from the nuns with you and to reveal how their ways are applicable to your relationship whether you've just started dating or have been married for a long time. The lessons in this book will allow you to garner much respect from your partner and to become well-admired. You will receive guidance on how to overcome obstacles in your marriage which will lead to less arguments in your life and more fulfilment overall. The bond you share with your loved one will strengthen as each chapter helps you navigate through the messiness of relationships. Getting along with someone can be extremely difficult, but the methods provided here will undoubtedly help you succeed.

The journey in this book begins with my continued pursuit of trying to become a nun and ends with my life as a married woman. The lessons that make up this book are based on real examples I took from my own experiences in order to make them the most practical and useful for you. I document each difficulty I encountered and how I overcame them, using the wisdom gleaned from the temple. Although I don't always directly reference the nuns in every lesson, their ideologies have heavily influenced my thinking and behaviors. Their spirits have been integrated into every facet of my daily practice. May their ways of peace and gentleness serve to benefit your life in every way.

1

The Sky

One of the fondest memories of my life is hanging laundry on the rooftop of my boarding school in Yun Lin, Taiwan. After I was denied entrance into the nunnery, I did not give up on my dream of becoming a nun. Instead, I lived in Taiwan for several more years, teaching in a religious educational community affiliated with my temple. I was hoping to get noticed by the sisters and have a second chance at my dream. For 329 out of 365 days a year, I communed with teachers and students alike in a place that was nicknamed "Edu Park." Nearly every day after work, I would go up to the rooftop of my dormitory to hang my newly washed clothes. It was always so dark and still up there, a perfect retreat from the hustle and bustle of everyday school life. I always felt so serene walking between the rows and rows of hanging, damp shirts. The warm light of the moon was always visible from up there and it never ceased to put me at ease after a long day. From such a high platform, I could see a lot of things; the tops of other buildings and even the dim flicker of city lights beyond the fields which surrounded our campus. Sometimes, friends or dorm mates would accompany me to the roof just to chat or to relieve the day's happenings. One particular time, a teacher and I were standing against the cement-wall bordering the edge. Together, we happily enjoyed the sounds of insects calling out into the night and gazed at the dark sky laden with shadowy clouds. She told me, "You know? I often look up at the stars and pray for my heart to be just as vast as the sky. I pray that my heart can love without boundaries just like the sky exists without boundaries." I took in her words and watched the stars twinkle. Suddenly there was a sweet silence that permeated the air between us. I was thinking about what she said and how it was such a lovely way to view things. Her words lingered around for a while, then drifted off into the expanse. But that moment changed a lot of things. I never saw the sky the same way again. I loved her prayer and tucked it away deep into my heart that night.

To this day, I still find myself mulling over her words in my mind when I'm going about my marriage from day to day. Whenever possible, I like to go out into the garden late at night, much like that night many years ago, and wait until the peace has settled in like a fog. Then I just look up into the mysterious expanse and imagine that my heart is growing just as wide as the space above. Her voice echoes in my mind. "I pray that my heart can be just as vast as the sky." Then, my own voice chimes in. "I also wish to take on many things in life and not let little things bother me. I hope to take on my husband's burdens whenever possible, both physical and emotional. Please help me absorb the world's troubles."

Whenever I find myself losing patience or feeling anger arising within, I often refer to that one special night where a lady shared a beautiful thought with me. It has made me a better wife.

2

Hitting a Low

I remember when I first embarked on the journey to Edu Park alone, I was so miserable when I arrived because I was incredibly homesick. At that point, it truly dawned on me that I had left *everything* behind. I was starting a new chapter utterly alone and the journey was much harder than expected. For the first several weeks, I wallowed in my own pain. I constantly thought about my suffering and reminded myself of everything I missed in America. To make matters worse, it was hot, humid and sticky where I was. It was incredibly uncomfortable just being there. It seemed like nothing was going right.

One evening, I went to attend a lecture and sat in my chair like a lifeless soul. The speaker was talking enthusiastically, but I had no interest. I stared into space and felt myself go numb. Halfway through, a thought suddenly hit me. "Shani, get up! Lift yourself up!" Intrigued, I kept listening. "There are many other lonely souls in the school too and not just you. You're in a boarding school for crying out loud. Everyone is lonely, you are not unique in this." In the depths of my despair, a forceful but understanding voice was trying to open me up to change. It was showing me all the great possibilities I could be a part of if I could just remove myself from my own misery. To an outsider, it probably looked like I was just sitting there, but much was being done inside my mind. My eyes were wide and alert as new ideas were forming. I was undergoing a transformation.

Afterwards, while still sitting in my chair, I suddenly felt a miraculous urge to get active and to make a positive change. I was filled with a renewed spirit. I wanted to seek out all the other lonely souls around me and to actually do something for them. Instead of wallowing in my own self-pity, I wanted to alleviate the pain of those around me. Was it a messenger waking me up? Or a stronger side of my conscience taking over? Whatever it was, it turned a giant force of sorrow into a greater force of passion. That night, I couldn't sleep because I was bubbling over with ideas on what I could do the next day.

Later, I found that this type of mysterious intervention would continue to occur in my life. I learned to recognize those moments because they seemed almost supernatural. Whenever I hit rock bottom from an argument with my husband or felt in my heart that "I could never forgive him this time," the sudden inspiration for change would always come sooner or later. I would feel a distinct strength rise from within and urge me to turn things around no matter how bad they had been.

Through those times, I have learned that each moment holds so much power. A person can be reborn in any given moment, even in those moments that seem devoid of all hope. Inspiration often comes when least expected. So don't be discouraged if you've hit a low. Sometimes, it is necessary to experience that state in order for something greater to manifest. Sometimes, it is precisely in that moment when you surrender that the inspiration comes. Pain is often the greatest catalyst for beauty. Just stay where you are and allow yourself to be receptive to anything. Be patient with yourself. When you are at your lowest, you are open to the greatest change.

3

Space

When I was intensely pursuing my path as a nun, the universe suddenly introduced James, my current husband, into my life and I was thrust into the deepest struggle of my life. I loved him but also felt that I had to continue my spiritual walk, which didn't involve him. It was a very painful experience to let go of the bond I felt with him. Even after I moved to a different country, I was not successful in letting him go and still maintained contact with him all the while. Years later, when I finally came to the realization that becoming a nun wasn't meant for me in this life, I went back home to America and started my life again from there.

Eventually, I married James and felt an overwhelming appreciation towards him. I appreciated the fact that he allowed me enough freedom to pursue my dream even when it didn't involve him. He was loving enough to let me go because he wanted me to be happy. It demonstrated volumes about his character. If he had been forceful and required me to stay with him no matter what, we probably wouldn't be together today. But his sacrifice of letting me go in order to follow my heart made me fall harder in love with him in the end.

People who are mature in love understand the importance of allowing others the space to find their happiness under any circumstance. They genuinely care about the wellbeing of that person and want them to have everything their heart desires. James didn't get upset and bitter over the fact that I left his side. He didn't sever all ties and tell me he never wanted to see me again because I had other ambitions. Instead, he told me that he would keep patiently waiting and that if it was meant to be, nothing could stop us from being together. His approach to the entire situation impressed me and I felt a greater respect for him through it all. He showed me what true love is all about; releasing the one you love out of selflessness and putting their needs above your own. He proved that his heart was in the right place, and by doing so, led me directly back to him.

4

Sweeping

Several times, I lived in the temple for a short while and learned alongside the nuns. They had very beautiful ways of seeing the world and I always felt inspired by their different outlooks. Even the most mundane tasks took on new meaning when the nuns were involved. Take the simple act of sweeping for example. A nun told me that when they sweep, they imagine they are sweeping away the negativity of their minds: impatience, irritability, greed, anger and the like. Cleaning the floor becomes a process of inner purification. With each speck of dirt they remove, they imagine the mind and heart being cleansed at the same time. In this way, sweeping becomes an active form of meditation. With outwardly actions, they are shaping their internal landscapes.

I liked the idea of this very much. I took the idea home with me and started implementing this concept whenever I did my chores. I imagined my house to be the inside of my mind and happily cleared away all the impurities. I put this teaching to use when I wiped the windows, scrubbed the toilets, and mopped the floors. Every dirty surface suddenly became an opportunity for my advancement.

How is this applicable to your relationship? Well, when you purify your soul, you are less likely to be filled with impatience, anger and hatred. If, on a daily basis, you work on removing the "dirtiness" of your mind, you will only emerge more beautiful and pure. This is the perfect platform to build the rest of your relationship on. As a calmer, lighter and happier person, you will engage in more peaceful conduct with your loved one. There will be less room in your heart for unpleasantness and peace will grow in your home like a well-nurtured flower.

5

Tears

The nuns taught me to practice non-violence and to be genuine which actually worked out very well for me because my husband is a tough guy; he doesn't respond well to harshness. He'll beat me at being tough every time. Through the years, I've found something that softens him up and dissolves his aggression faster than anything else. Crying. He hates to see me cry and always backs down when I do. He responds to the softer approach that I was taught and actually wants to protect me when I show my vulnerability. I never meant to cry on purpose in front of him, but doing so allowed me to find a better way of communicating with him.

I also found crying to be effective in other areas of my life and not just my marriage. For example, one semester when I was teaching at Edu Park, I was to teach the most difficult class on campus. It was a sixth-grade class full of boys. Supposedly, the students were ruthless and cruel to any teacher brave enough to step foot into their classroom. No one could handle them up to that point. And as an ambitious newcomer, I volunteered myself for the undesirable position.

I went in to teach this particular class not knowing what to expect and found that the rumors were not an exaggeration. Papers were flying everywhere when I walked into the classroom and students were running around, doing whatever they pleased. It was chaos. It was difficult to get anyone's attention no matter what I tried. At one point, someone stood up and cussed at me from across the room. I was in disbelief. After several weeks of failing miserably to conduct any type of class whatsoever, I felt so dejected. Without knowing what else to do, I sat down in my chair one day in front of the students and just started crying. Yes, I started crying. I just let it all out. The amazing thing is, *that* finally got their attention. They had never seen a teacher cry in front of them before.

When I was able to speak, I told them how much I missed my family and friends in America. I told them how hard it was for me to make the transition from the U.S. to Taiwan and how even the weather was something I couldn't get used to. Lastly, I revealed how their behavior was causing a lot of stress to me on top of everything I had to deal with. I let myself become completely vulnerable and transparent to them. I just laid out all my difficulties as if they were my companions and asked for their help in easing my troubles by behaving better. Miraculously, everyone was dead silent and listening with complete attention.

That was the turning point of my relationship with them. Their hearts somehow softened from my sharing and the following week, they were complete little angels, waiting for me to come in and teach them. When I revealed the softness in me, they took down their walls. They responded to my gentleness with more gentleness. When I shared my struggles, it struck a chord in them because they were most likely suffering as well. Exposing our true selves can be so affective in communicating with others without causing any damage. It breaks down all the walls and connects people at a heart level. Practice being completely real and uninhibited. It will bring out the most effective and compassionate response from others.

6

Negative Support

We often hear people talking about the importance of giving *positive support* to our loved ones; building them up and encouraging them on their endeavors. But rarely, do we hear about giving *negative support* which is just as important. The notion was first introduced to me by my uncle who belonged to the same religious group as me. Sitting on the couch, he told me, "People sometimes need negative support, which means being able to stay with them as they experience low moods; staying with them even when they act ugly and undesirable. Negative support means remaining steady and calm even when the person is breaking down due to their pain. To be able to act as a crutch to them as they go through such hard times is an extraordinary gift."

I can think of several times in my life where I've needed negative support. During those times, I was always in a lot of pain, confusion and frustration. One time, I was home for winter break from being in Edu Park for half a year. My parents expected me to come back from my first semester as an angel, washed clean of the world's ugliness. To their knowledge, being submerged in such a sacred environment would change me for the better. But when I came home, I was quite the opposite. I acted terribly and was quick to anger at them. I was unstable and irritable. Confused, my mom secretly spoke to the head monk of the school and asked about my weird behavior. He told her that my behavior was actually normal and common for the students in the school. During the school year, everyone underwent a lot of hardships from being away from home. Everyone struggled and held things inside for many months. So going home to a place of comfort and familiarity naturally allowed all of those negative feelings to be expelled.

What he said was very true. I held in a lot of negative emotions during the school year because I had to support my students who were also struggling. When I finally came back home, all of my pent-up negativity was hurled at my family. I needed their negative support as I broke down. As I reflect on the people who have shown me this type of support, I am beyond thankful to them. I couldn't handle my pain in any other way and feel so grateful for their willingness to accept me in my terrible state.

It's not easy to be the bearer of negative support in marriage. You have to be completely overcome by love for this person. You need to be skillful enough to remove yourself from how things appear and just be there to catch the other person when they fall. You must delve deeper into the scenario and remember that this situation is not personal. The person in front of you is ailing in some way and needs help. If you can do this, you will have achieved something extremely difficult.

This extraordinary act of love will be recognized and cherished from the recipient's heart. For myself, I have never forgotten the people that demonstrated this selfless act to me. Because of them, I know how critical it is to receive negative support and how rare it is to find people willing to supply it.

7

Flaws

When I lived in Taiwan, my body had a hard time adjusting to the climate and it showed on my face. I had the worst acne of my life! Red bumps covered my entire face. This was rather embarrassing because I couldn't hide my face and it was the first thing people saw when they talked to me.

Even after I returned to the States years later and my condition improved, my complexion was still nowhere near perfect and I would always wish my skin was better. When I saw girls who had perfect skin, I could never suppress that twinge of envy. I often wished I could look more like them because I thought that was the definition of beautiful.

However, one day, after watching a gorgeous model on TV, my thinking changed. I suddenly realized that it's easy to be attracted to someone who's flawless and perfect. It's effortless; anyone can do it. But when someone can be attracted to another person despite their flaws and love them for who they are, then that is a demonstration of real love. I told myself, I'm not perfect, but James still loves me. He loves me despite my imperfections. I don't have a perfect figure, the best complexion, or the best personality. But the more imperfections I have, the more genuine and sweet his love becomes. They're like tests to show me he can look past superficial qualities and love the real me.

As a conclusion, I don't have to constantly compare myself to other girls who are better than me. My husband loves me just the way I am and that's a pretty nice thought.

8

Fight

Yes, you read that right. Go ahead and fight! That might sound weird coming from someone who aspired to be a nun but I believe true benefits can come about from fighting.

During my time at Edu Park, I sometimes heard people yelling at each other in the school. This behavior puzzled me because Edu Park was supposed to have the atmosphere of a temple; peaceful and quiet. Why would people be so undisciplined and fight each other in such a place? After witnessing this several more times, I finally asked an older and wiser teacher about it. "Isn't it bad for people to fight here?" I asked her bluntly. "We're in a sacred place." Her response surprised me.

"It may seem that way, but actually I believe there is merit in fighting. At least those people are communicating and finally being honest with each other. They're getting their *real* views across. And only then can they move towards finding a peaceful solution."

I had never viewed fighting in such a way before. Ever since I was a kid, fighting had always been against the rules. It was associated with bad behavior. But here in this holy place, someone was showing me that fighting could actually be a means to peace; a part of a journey that is not complete yet. I found it very interesting.

Years after that incident had passed, I reconnected with an old friend from high school. We were at the beach, sitting happily on the sand. She asked me how my new married life was and I revealed to her quite honestly how sometimes my husband and I fight. I even admitted to becoming a monster at times, screaming and yelling and even throwing things. "My behavior always leaves me embarrassed because I try to be good all the time," I finished. Once again, her stance on things surprised me.

"Shani, in high school you always kept your emotions locked away inside. Whenever I asked you how you were doing, you would reply 'Fine,' even when it was obvious you weren't fine. I always felt that you were holding in so many things and that it was so damaging to your health. Now when you tell me you turn crazy in front of James, I actually feel relieved for you. You found someone you feel comfortable enough with to reveal all your sides to. You must truly trust him and have confidence in him. That leads me to believe that you two have a good relationship."

When she finished her comment, I was shocked. I thought to myself: "What? I just told her that I become a monster when we fight and she told me we have a good relationship?" That was not what I expected to hear. But at the same time, I could see what she meant. Revealing everything to someone requires a deep form of trust, perhaps a trust I never had with anyone else. And expressing pain is far better than repressing it in the long run. It was pretty nice that there was someone I could express every facet of myself to and, at the same time, know that he would not leave me.

With the help of my two friends' insightful thinking, I realized that bad things aren't always bad; they often result in something good.

Communicating is always better than not communicating. So if you must, go ahead and fight. Tell them what you really think. I have confidence that good results can always come out of every circumstance.

9

Shaved Head

When I stayed with the nuns, I noticed that many of them had the habit of running their hands over their shaved heads first thing in the morning. It would still be dark outside and they would sit up in bed, rubbing their heads with their eyes closed. I didn't understand what it meant until I asked one of the nuns one day. Apparently, that gesture serves to remind them of the reason why they chose the difficult path of becoming a nun in the first place. By rubbing their heads, they are reminded of why they cut off all their hair and left the worldly life behind them. The drastic act of giving up everything was performed for a purpose very close to their heart. Perhaps they wanted to find true happiness or develop compassion to help all living beings. Whatever the reason, it is important that they not lose sight of it, otherwise it would be too much of a waste to have come this far and then not remember.

Rubbing their heads is a way for them to set their intentions for the day and to prepare their mind. They have to center themselves and keep their target in mind. That way, everything they do during the day can help them get closer to their goal.

I find that this ritual of mind-setting is equally important in my life as well. Although I'm not living in a temple, I find it essential to set my intentions for the day and to prepare my heart in the right direction. Otherwise, I'll just be swept away by the activities of the day and not even know why I am doing anything; much like a leaf being blown around in the wind. If I set some time aside every morning to remind myself of the *light* I wish to be, then I step out into the world with concentrated focus and achieve more in every moment. My actions start to serve my purpose and nothing gets wasted. I find that I also become more patient and loving to deal with family members and other people I come across, as I remind myself every morning of the kind of person I want to become. I encourage you to set your intentions every day. Do not underestimate the power of this exercise as it can make all the difference in where you're going.

10

Criticism

During my time in Asia, I heard from James that it was very hard to get a job in the States. He, himself, had been to several interviews and was unable to successfully land a position. Finally, through the help of a friend, he obtained a job answering emails at a company. Before long, his work ethic caught the attention of his boss and he effortlessly rose up to become an upper-level manager in no time. I was not at all surprised because I knew that James has a sharp and intelligent mind that would quickly be recognized by those in leadership positions.

There are many benefits I've enjoyed as a result of my husband's cleverness. But one area I've struggled with is receiving his criticisms well. He is so observant and sharp that he often catches my mistakes or wants to show me how to do something better. Whenever this happened in the past, I would feel anxious and unhappy at having been corrected.

My whole mind would struggle against it and I would take his words in a negative way.

This situation was really starting to bother me so one day I decided to do as the nuns do and reflect internally on the matter. I knew that I held the answers within. After much contemplation, it dawned on me why I always had such a strong reaction from being criticized. It's because I was so lacking in self-love that I was constantly thirsting for praise and approval from others. I was seeking validation and love through other people because I couldn't find those things within myself. I needed others to see my value in order for me to be convinced that I was valuable. Therefore, I people-pleased and did everything I could to prove my worth all the time. I put my best out there and acted in ways that I thought others would like.

As a result, when someone criticized me, I took it as a very hard blow. The words would crush me. To me, being criticized felt like I wasn't being loved. I was a failure and my best efforts weren't good enough.

When I realized what was going on, I knew I had to change my relationship with myself. I really needed to start loving myself from within and seeing my own magnificence. I was a product of the universe and was made perfect in my own way. I didn't need to be so harsh on myself or try so hard to put on an act for others to like me. I was wonderful the way I was. I just had to see it myself first and really embrace my uniqueness.

Also, when people criticized me, it didn't mean that they didn't love me anymore. I was just taking it the wrong way. Criticisms could actually be helpful and time-saving as there are often ways to do a thing better. In the end, it all came down to how I viewed myself. I needed to work on directing my love inwards instead of seeking it outward. That's how I finally freed myself from the disappointment of being criticized;

realizing that words did not create or take away from my value. I was already valuable.

11

Just Say It

When I was little, I was terribly shy and didn't talk much. Perhaps growing up in an Asian family didn't help either since everyone was quite reserved and didn't express their feelings very openly. "I love you," was rarely spoken and during upsetting times, retreating to one's own room was more the norm. I never learned to talk through a problem or to communicate properly. Much of what I felt was always buried deep within my heart and never revealed. I suppressed many things and this only intensified as I got older.

As an adult, I had a friend who was always late to our outings. I'm talking about an hour or so late each time. Whenever she finally arrived, I would pretend like it didn't bother me and that everything was okay. I didn't want to start any conflicts with her. But actually, it was grating on me inside. For years, I kept silent. One day, we were to meet on Christmas Eve to exchange presents. I got there on time, as usual, and she was about an hour and thirty minutes late. To make things worse, I was seven months pregnant and very hormonal. That time, I had *finally* had enough. I couldn't contain my anger anymore and I blew up at her. I was completely rude and hostile. We became very bitter and haven't spoken to each other since.

It wasn't until later when my spiritual teacher prompted us to work at being better communicators that something opened up inside of me. "If something bothers you, just say it!" she would coax us. She was telling us that it was okay to express ourselves and that we *should*; it's a normal process of fostering healthy relationships. Things changed slowly after I heard her message because I wanted to practice her teaching and work at becoming better.

Now, when I look back on what happened with my friend, I wish I had handled things differently. I wish I had implemented what my teacher taught me and told her from the beginning that her tardiness bothered me. I wish I had just let it out when it was a small sprout. But instead, I waited until that sprout had grown into a fearsome beanstalk and it finally burst through the roof with its sheer power. Because of my inability to communicate properly, I lost a good friend that day.

It's true that I was more shy and quiet than the average person. But still, I know a lot of people who keep things inside and don't communicate their true feelings. I knew a couple once who actually avoided speaking to each other for two months while living under the same roof. It seems like such a torture to live in that kind of suffocating environment for so long. It's hard on both parties. The wife said she was too proud to talk about her feelings to her husband. But what I wish she realized was that: holding it all in just makes everything worse and makes you suffer so much. Most likely the other person doesn't even know that particular thing is bothering you. Therefore, whenever there is something on your mind, practice letting it out. Don't let it grow. Don't be like who I was and hold everything inside. There's nothing good that comes out of suppressing your emotions. If there's something on your mind, just say it. Don't block the road of communication. Trust that you will feel much better when both of you openly express how you truly feel.

12

Just Say It (Cont.)

It's one thing to just say something. But what is the next step? How does one eventually go on to communicate more skillfully? It may seem complicated, but it's actually all very easy. Communication is simply allowing each person to see each other's point of view. Everyone grew up in a different reality. Everyone's world is so different, but often we forget that and expect others to think just like we do. When others don't and act in ways that are contrary to our beliefs, it's easy to get upset and judgmental. From there, arguments tend to arise in a hostile manner.

For example, one day James got upset at me because I didn't clean out the condiments on the side of the fridge. There were bottles and bottles of everything you could think of. Some of them were no longer being used and had even expired. With each bottle he had to throw out, he was getting frustrated. "Hadn't we decided that she would take care of this?" he fumed inside. In his reality, I was not doing my job. I was giving him more work to do when he was busy already. He had grown up with a fridge that was always spotless and free of clutter. Therefore, it bothered him to see such a mess.

In my reality, however, things were different. I grew up with a fridge that was always cluttered with no one knowing what was lurking in the back. The fridge was like a mysterious void, often harboring things from the past. James didn't realize that I was already making an attempt to keep our current fridge clean to his standards, despite my different upbringing. The main shelves were clean, I had just missed the side door. What he also didn't realize was that I don't like to waste anything. If something is still usable, I find it a pity to throw it away. That's why some of the bottles still kept their place on the shelf.

James and I both had different realities. We were standing on different islands. Therefore, we had to build a bridge to allow each person to understand where the other was coming from. We had to *communicate*. I took the reins and started by explaining to him that I was not trying to neglect my duties or to give him a hard time. I had simply spent my whole life growing up with a different set of habits. Piece by piece, we had to reveal the pictures of our lives until both parties could come to an understanding and proceed more calmly and compassionately. Communication is simply allowing dialogue to *flow*.

People who are not skilled in communicating tend to hold things inside, act passive aggressively or give the silent treatment. However, choosing not to communicate blocks the road and prevents the bridge from building. It leaves each person stranded on their own island. Try to be the one that helps the other person along. Help them understand where you're coming from and allow them to express themselves so that you can understand as well. Marriage was not designed to be two separate islands, but just one. Communication is the vehicle that can get you there.

13

Generosity

When I was little, I often had strong urges to give things to others, be it letters, trinkets, presents or whatever I had on hand. It was just so innate to me. When I wasn't able to give, I would feel very bothered and think of everything I could to find a way.

Sometimes I would revert to extreme measures and get myself into trouble. For example, one time when I was five, I wanted to buy a gift for my kindergarten teacher. It must have been around Christmas time and I wanted to get her something pretty. My mom said no though, and I was very upset. That should've been the end of that. But, I was so determined to give something to my teacher that I went against my better judgement and stole some earrings from the stash of jewelry my mom was selling. I thought one little pair of earrings wouldn't make a difference to her big collection and slipped them into a gift box. Later, the box was delivered into my teacher's hands by my own little hands and I was grinning from ear to ear.

My deed was soon found out though. My teacher personally returned the earrings to my mom shortly after, saying she did not have pierced ears and therefore couldn't wear them. My mom was puzzled, saying she hadn't remembered giving any earrings to her. My face turned red all the while. The truth was soon uncovered. When I got home, I deserved all that was coming for me.

I'm not proud of what I did, but that instance just illustrates how badly I wanted to give and how frustrated I felt when I didn't have the means. It was almost painful for me not to give when I wanted to. Perhaps it was because I already recognized the benefits of giving even at my early age. I saw how happy it made people and how they seemed to appreciate it with their whole hearts. Through my young eyes, I had already seen people moved to the point of tears from receiving something and I marveled at such a phenomenon. Giving seemed so easy to do, yet it was able to produce such strong and positive results. Witnessing the joy that giving brought filled me with such satisfaction and I felt myself wanting to give everything to everyone.

Throughout my life, that same sensation has stayed with me. But thankfully, I became much more equipped to give than I had been in the past. After I came into contact with the nuns, I found that my practice was actually not that far off from theirs. The nuns actively give away everything they own, not leaving even a single hair on their heads. They reserve all good things for others and live very simply themselves. They are perhaps the most generous givers on Earth.

One of the things I loved most about James while dating him was his generosity. When we went to the movies, he would spoil me with popcorn, candy and drinks, all in the largest sizes available. He acted like money wasn't an object to him as long as I was involved and that just made him so lovable to me. I appreciated his generous nature which made me feel so special. His heart was so big in that regard. It's hard not to fall in love with someone so giving and spoiling. He wasn't rich but he had a rich heart.

On the other hand, I've seen people who are miserly and stingy. What they don't realize is that people respond to you the way you are to them. If you are stingy to your family and friends, then they'll be stingy right back to you. They won't want to do anything extra for you. But if you keep a wide-open heart and give generously, then everyone will feel so grateful and think of you whenever they have something good. They will want to shower you with love and everything they have. Isn't that a more fortunate and desirable route?

14

Generosity (Cont.)

Although I consider myself a rather giving person, I have also seen my heart become closed off in particular situations. For example, on one occasion, I decided to do a random act of kindness for a friend and to send her some stationary. She had just posted a picture online of a hand-written card and the image inspired me to put a package together for her. I bundled up an assortment of cards and stickers and tied them up together with string. I wrapped it all up in brown paper and decorated the outside of it. I tried to make it look as cheerful as I could, then mailed it out to her right away. For weeks after, I never heard back from her. She never even confirmed that she had received my gift.

Negative thoughts started to arise in my mind. I thought, "She is so ungrateful. I shouldn't have gone through the trouble to do that for her." But before my thoughts could go any further, I suddenly realized how my motivation for giving was all wrong. I was giving for the sake of receiving something back—a good word, a compliment, a reaction. And when I didn't get that, I regretted giving at all. That is not the true spirit of giving. Giving should always be done without thought of reward. Otherwise, it would simply be a transaction: I give to you, then you give to me. But what's the fun in that? The best way to approach giving is to do it solely for the satisfaction that it brings. Then, forget about it altogether. Don't hold onto the deed and linger on with expectations. Just let it go.

Shortly after my change of heart, my friend messaged me, thanking me for my thoughtful present. Apparently, she had been away during the holidays and only saw my package when she returned. I felt silly, but through the whole scenario, I also learned to give with better intentions. The whole event almost seemed pre-ordained, as I needed to learn that lesson and I felt thankful for the change it put me through.

15

Sensitivities

During the summer of third grade, I developed a new hairstyle for myself. It involved taking two strands of hair and strategically placing them over my eyes. To reinforce this look, I rubbed gel liberally on those strands so that they became like hardened sticks. Somehow, I thought I looked great. I went around sporting this new hairstyle for much of the school year. I was proud of how I looked, but some people didn't agree with my vision. They would make hurtful comments and sneer at me. No matter how I saw things though, I still thought I looked best in this way.

Over time, I became very sensitive with the topic of my hair and didn't like people making any mention of it. It would make me feel very uneasy and embarrassed. A friend of mine didn't know I had developed a sensitivity towards my hair and she started making fun of me one day. She said the strands on my face looked like cockroach antennas. I tried to play it off at first, pretending like her comments didn't affect me. But the more she rubbed it in, the more furious and ashamed I felt. I finally burst into tears (having my pride wounded so badly) and have never forgotten the incidence since.

What I learned from my guru (and what turned out to be true for myself) is that almost everyone you meet will have a certain quality that they're sensitive about, be it their weight, their acne, their relationship status, height, etc. If you are someone's spouse, then you are probably very much aware of what your spouse's sensitivities are.

Although it may be tempting to bring those up during an argument, especially to spite your spouse or to push their buttons, try to make all effort to avoid doing so. It can be very damaging to their confidence and leave irreparable damage that you will later regret. Keep others' feelings in mind and don't resort to behavior that will bring them great pain in the long run. Whenever possible, try your hardest to avoid others' sensitivities. Your carefulness with their feelings will be profoundly appreciated and reciprocated.

16

Good Practitioner

When I was 26, I traveled to Prince Edward Island to visit one of our temples there and also to attend religious classes. It was such a treat to travel to such an exotic location because it was for spiritual learning and hey, spiritual learning isn't often associated with fun and travel. I almost felt guilty for studying in such a picturesque place but I got over that quickly.

Every week, I attended classes led by monks and always looked forward to them. Those classes were important to me at the time because I was going through a lot in my personal life and really needed guidance. After each class, I would go up to the monks to seek additional advice. I told them about my problems and how I was trying to overcome them. One day, in the midst of my sharing, a monk made an unexpected comment to me. Instead of telling me how I could've done things better, he simply said, "You are a good practitioner."

His words were the last thing I expected to hear, given all the struggles I had just told him. But I felt the curious spark of hope that his words sent through me. I couldn't believe a well-respected monk felt that way about me. I was on air. His words ignited something in my heart and suddenly, I had something to live up to. He said I was a good practitioner and I was going to prove him right. His confidence in my abilities meant everything to me.

Many years later, his encouragement still helps me through difficulties. When I feel I am being falsely accused by my husband or that I want to yell back during an argument, I feel those words coming through: "You are a good practitioner." They stop me in my tracks and make me rethink how I want to proceed. I am reminded that I cannot be so easily defeated by shortcomings because there is someone who believes in me. When I want to leave the house in a fit of rage or say something utterly mean and full of hatred, I remember that I am a good practitioner so I cannot be so destructive. That simple phrase has given me unbelievable power to overcome numerous hurdles.

Now, I'd also like to say to you that you, my friend, are a good practitioner. You have the power. You have light and peace inside of you. You are an oasis of peace and a child of the benevolent. There is nothing you cannot overcome and there is so much that you are capable of achieving. I believe in you. You are a good practitioner and you can do *anything*.

17

Words

There are many mysteries to me in the world. One of them happens to be myself. I've struggled to understand the two sides of me that exist. One is infinitely obedient, gentle, patient and nun-like. The other side is bold, daring and always craving excitement.

At one point in my life, I learned how to ride a motorcycle because I wanted to race on the freeway at high speeds. Around the same time,

I wanted to become a nun and stay locked up in a temple forever. Both desires seem so contradictory yet I've always had to juggle between the two personalities that make up who I am.

Perhaps that is why I was drawn to my husband who was so rebellious when I first met him. I saw him several times at religious events, usually to pick up his mom and never there for his own sake. He was always smoking and looking too cool for anyone. One time, it seems he was somehow persuaded to stay for lunch. During that time, I caught a glimpse of him staring angrily at his vegetarian sandwich. I'll never forget the look on his face. It was full of disgust and shock, as if he was saying, "Ew! What is this? How can they serve me this?" He was such a difficult one, but somehow I was drawn to him. Perhaps his rebellious nature excited me.

When my mom found out I was dating him, she feared for my life because he was over six feet tall and looked like a gangster. She forbade me from seeing him, but that was not enough to deter us. I didn't want to disobey her but I also couldn't resist the attraction I felt towards him.

Over the next five years, I had to do a lot of convincing on my mom. (*A lot*). I knew this guy was who I wanted to be with. Although he had a rough exterior, I sensed something within him that was good and almost pure; a contradiction, much like myself. He had a lot of good qualities that were worth fighting for and now, it was just up to me to show my mom what I saw. If I had learned anything from the nuns, it was that the power of positive speech could melt away any barriers- words have a way of bringing about great transformation in others. So I set about the whole process with determination.

It was not easy at first because my mom was so set in her beliefs about James. But I didn't care. I just kept praising his good qualities and emphasizing the nice things he did as much as I could. Day after day, I preached his strengths while muting his flaws, or choosing not to bring them up altogether. I never left out any detail of his goodness if I knew it would help my argument. And then, years later, like a plant that's been constantly watered, my mom finally learned to respect and admire this man she used to fear.

Through this whole ordeal, I saw first-hand that our words go a long way. We can influence those around us so much just by the words we choose to speak. Everything we say can influence someone even if the results aren't always visible immediately. The seeds we plant with our speech *always* bear fruit in due time. And thus, I believe we must wield our power of speech wisely. When we speak positively about others, we bring people together. We bring peace and harmony to the forefront. Go ahead and be the one to set an example. Be the bridge that connects everyone together.

18

Bugs

When I was 13, my cousin started exploring religion. She became increasingly intrigued by the teachings she heard and would often share stories with me. I enjoyed her stories quite a bit. One topic that especially captivated me was animals and how they are often mistreated in society. According to her, animals have feelings too and do not wish to suffer any more than we do. Every creature deserves respect. Soon after hearing all of those new concepts, my point of view on living beings changed dramatically. When I saw my friends squash bugs because they were scared of them or throw snails onto the street for fun, I felt uneasy about it. I had been guilty of doing similar things in the past. But now these acts seemed more and more cruel to me. I started to wonder, "Just because something is smaller than me, does that mean I can kill it?"

A thought also occurred to me one day—if dinosaurs were still alive and shared the planet with us, we would appear to be just like ants to them. They could easily squash us and assume that we don't have feelings. But is that right? Just like any creature, we desire to live and to avoid pain. Size is not an acceptable reason for killing if you ask me.

I understand a lot of people don't share my thinking. My husband was one of them. When he first saw me escorting bugs in our house outside by means of a plastic cup or paper towel, he would often shake his head. He thought I was being ridiculous. However, I told myself that I would rather go through the trouble and be made fun of than to just let those bugs die. They were precious little creatures in my eyes and I wanted to follow through with my new belief. I continued on with my habit, year after year, all by myself.

One day, my husband and I decided to grab some lunch on our way home from the park. We parked in front of a pizza shop and my husband stayed behind in the car while I went in to get our food. When I came back out, my husband was excited to tell me something he had just witnessed.

"There was a little girl who came out of that store right there," he started. "She was about ten years old with blond hair. Anyway, she ran all the way over to the bushes by our car. She didn't see me, but I saw that she was unwrapping a bug in a tissue. She was setting it free, just like you always do. That was so nice of her!"

He said it with such excitement and praise that I was thoroughly amused... and also a bit confused. Something had changed between the past and now. My husband's perception of saving bugs had changed. He used to think I was weird for doing it, but now, he got excited watching someone else do it. I learned a valuable lesson in that moment. His perception had begun to change over the years even though I was totally unaware. I first introduced the concept to him and although it was hard for him to accept it, he slowly familiarized himself with it every time I took a bug outside. The idea was refreshed in his mind repeatedly until it almost became natural. When he witnessed the same behavior being performed elsewhere, it solidified his new belief and triggered his enthusiasm. In the end, he supported the idea without even knowing what hit him.

My message to you is this. Stand your ground on your own noble beliefs and don't be discouraged by other people's initial comments. Don't give up your values because of disapproval you may receive. If you feel in your heart that what you are doing is right, keep pressing onward and more often than not, the idea will grow on others eventually and allow them to see things in a new light. By continuing to practice what you believe is virtuous, you will influence others to be better and to help them exercise their better judgement.

19

The Treasure

I had quite a few male pursuers after I became a teenager. Several of them tried to kiss me at one point but I could never allow myself to be kissed by any of them. One particular memory stands out in my mind. A guy came to visit me at my house one night and I met him outside, wearing my childish pajamas. As he was leaving, he closed his eyes and leaned in towards me as if to kiss me. I was totally caught unawares and panicked. I didn't want to kiss him back. But what was I to do? He was leaning in already. So I did the only thing I could think to do in that moment. I let out a little yelp. Yes, you read that right. I yelped. His eyes flashed open, he was obviously startled. Then he started apologizing profusely and we awkwardly parted ways. I still cringe when I think about how I reacted. It's so embarrassing. But I hadn't developed any feelings for him at all and simply didn't feel comfortable locking lips with a stranger.

Perhaps it was my mom's influence that made me so cautious with myself and with my body. She always taught me that I should make myself expensive and not give myself away to just any guy that comes along. Her belief seems to align with the nuns' belief that the body is a sacred temple and a vessel for all things holy. It should not be misused or disregarded, but should be treasured and protected most carefully. Although nuns do not partake in romantic relations with men, I found that their point of view still helped me in my relationships. I treated my body like it was a treasure and guarded it until I found someone worthy enough to earn it. I could also hear my mom's voice saying, "If you give yourself away to men so easily, you will lose their respect and become cheap to them. Getting physical right away may seem like it's what they want, but over time, it's not what they truly desire deep down. Men like women who are respectable and classy."

As it turns out, my very first kiss would be with my now-husband and even that kiss took almost two years to obtain. James really had the patience to wait around for me and I'm glad to say that it was the sweetest and most comfortable kiss I ever had. In the end, I'm glad I followed my mom's advice and waited for the right person to come along. I'm glad that I experienced some of life's sweetest moments with the one that really mattered because it made everything so much more special.

20

Agreements

I used to be the biggest flake. When people made plans with me, I would often cancel at the very last minute and make up some lame excuse. I never did it out of malice. I was simply too introverted to follow through with my plans sometimes. Whenever it came down to it, I always wanted to just stay home and relax in my pajamas, while reading or watching television.

During college, however, I went to hear a nun speak at the temple and she ignited a change in me. Her message for the night was regarding how important it is to stay true to our words and to be credible. According to her, the only thing we can truly give others is our word. If we don't follow through with our words, then what have we given them?

For some reason, the words of the nun had quite an impact on me that night. I walked away from the event thinking about all the people I had given empty words to. I had not been a person of credibility, but quite the opposite. I had let so many people down and disappointed others time and time again. I wanted to make a change. Starting that day, I put forth a real effort to really follow through with my words. If I made plans with someone, I made sure to keep them. If I told someone I'd call them back later, I'd do it. I'd start keeping my word to the minutest of details. If the sales clerk asked me to do a survey for them and I agreed, I made sure to put a note about it on my phone so that I could actually do it later.

With time, I became very conscious of the words I spoke and of the things I agreed to. I tried to never let a thing slip by which I had agreed to. I haven't always succeeded but I'm happy to say that now, I feel a lot more responsible. I feel good knowing that I'm not letting others down and that my words carry weight. By understanding the importance of the agreements I give, I have become a more trustworthy, reliable and thoughtful person to those I love. People have responded likewise in a positive manner and I can sense their appreciation. It just makes for a more pleasant interaction all around.

21

Exchanging Suffering

For some reason, I became fixated on suffering as a young adult. I recognized that people everywhere suffered every day and as long as that fact remained, I needed to know what that suffering was like for them. It didn't seem good enough to me if I was completely comfortable and others weren't. Often, I would subject myself to small doses of suffering just so I could imagine being in others' shoes and not get too comfortable where I was. I'd sometimes walk in the bitter cold without a jacket or go long stretches of time without eating. I wanted to feel and relate to others' pain.

I must have freaked my sister out when, for her birthday, I bought her a book depicting gruesome events from the past. The book was complete with decapitated men and war-torn landscapes. Many pages were filled to the brim with pain.

I don't know what I was thinking. Maybe I thought she'd enjoy looking at significant historical events, despite their sometimes depressing nature, since she was a history major in college. But I only realized later how strange this must have been for her. Most people try to avoid suffering but I wanted to know it better.

Later, after I got better acquainted with the nuns, I found that they practiced something really beautiful that involved connecting one's personal suffering with others. Finally, there was a benefit to the dark trait I possessed. What the nuns would do is mentally take on the suffering of others when they themselves suffer. For example, if one of the nuns came down with a splitting headache, she would imagine that she was taking on the headaches for all living beings and suffering in place of them.

It is an exercise to relieve harm from others by putting it upon oneself and offering the greatest comfort to them instead. This mentality is aligned with the nun's wish to be completely selfless and for all beings to have happiness. Taking on such an exercise yields several benefits. For one, the pain at hand suddenly becomes so much more meaningful because you are not only suffering for yourself but also for all who exist. And two, your heart expands with compassion as you link yourself to all who experience similar situations in life.

I distinctly remember one night when I sat on the floor of the laundry room in our house with the lights out. My husband and I had just gotten into a huge fight and I was in so much pain. There, in the dark and on the floor, I suddenly thought of the nuns' practice. I thought of all the women who had ever been in my place. I thought of how broken and isolated they felt, like I was feeling then, and my heart wept for them. In fact, I felt such a well-spring of emotion that it was like I was cradling those women in my arms, understanding their hearts completely.

Although I was incredibly sad that night, I also felt that what I was going through connected me to other people and helped me derive meaning from my pain. I was understanding the hearts of those in the world with me and at the same time, vowing to take away their suffering. It changed my personal experience completely.

In the end, I find that there are no wasted experiences in life. Everything you go through can serve a much greater purpose. When you feel the range of negative and positive emotions, you bring yourself one step closer to knowing the hearts of every human being. Everything you go through, in essence, is beneficial to all. Therefore, live each moment with an awareness that you are not alone. Every circumstance you go through ties you deeper into the fabric of humanity and allows you to become strengthened in your connection to others.

22

Insecurity

My husband was my first boyfriend, and because I eventually married him, he was the only boyfriend I ever had. Sure, I had crushes in the past and even let a guy hold my hand once. But that was it. That's as far as my experiences went. However, this was not the case for James. James had loved someone before me and for the longest time, I couldn't find peace within myself for this. I didn't know what it was like to love someone else deeply like I was loving James at the moment. And to know that that person still existed on the planet? I often questioned if he still had feelings for her. It only seemed natural. Whenever I asked him, he would always scoff, reassuring me that he absolutely didn't. This was not enough to appease me though and I constantly felt uneasy over his past. Because of my insecurity and lack of understanding, I would always feel bothered and let myself toy with the possibility that my husband still had fragments of feelings reserved for her.

My sadness over this eventually consumed me and even kept me up some nights. It was tiresome. Yet, deep down, I felt perhaps I was being ridiculous. I had to get to the bottom of things; it was driving me crazy.

I started to really delve inwards to figure out how to solve my problem. I reflected deeply upon myself and tried to listen for answers. Several days later, it finally became clear to me.

My deep fear and insecurity over his fidelity had nothing to do with him or his past at all. It all had to do with *me*. I felt so bothered because I didn't see the worth in myself. I didn't consider myself valuable, and always thought that other people were better than me. So naturally, I thought it would be easy for him to love others more than he would love me. I didn't love myself and was projecting my views onto him.

The key to fixing this problem was to start loving myself and to start seeing my own worth. I had to make my self-image healthier and to stop the negative chatter in my head that constantly talked down upon myself. I needed to fully embrace who I was and say, "Heck! James is so darn lucky to have me."

One day, I was suddenly inspired to look for a photograph of James and me. I found one taken several years before which I felt really conveyed his affection for me. We were in a car and he was leaning protectively into me. It is one of my favorite pictures to date. Even when I look at it now, I feel like his love for me in there is almost palpable; it's written in his eyes. I printed that picture out and put it by my bedside. If I woke up again in the night, I would just look over at the picture and be reminded that James loves me very much and drift back to sleep on that thought. Since that time, I have never really been bothered by James' past again. I have slept soundly and without obsessive thoughts.

In the end, I took back my own power by understanding that the cure to my own suffering is within me. Whenever *any* feelings of insecurity arose, it would always be my cue to stop and reflect how I am viewing myself. Most likely, I am not seeing myself in a positive light. The key to freedom is in me and not in my husband or in his previous girlfriends or in other women. *I* am the one I need to focus on. Feeling insecure is always a reminder for me to be more loving towards who I am. Only I can release myself from my own prison.

23

The Ruptured Appendix

Prayer is undoubtedly a huge part of the nuns' way of life. During my time with them, I saw that they often sought guidance through quiet prayer all throughout the day. I, myself, did not grow up with the habit of praying. But when I was 13, an event occurred in my life which changed me considerably. It all started on a regular Thursday night around Christmas time. I was suddenly struck with a terrible pain in my stomach which lasted several days. No one knew at the time, but I was experiencing a ruptured appendix that was killing me. We went to the hospital and the doctor examined me but diagnosed my pain as a harmless bout of gas. He told us we were free to go home and that I should just rest over the next couple of days. On our way out, however, a surgeon noticed how terrible I looked and wouldn't let me go home. According to him, my face was green and I needed to stay in the hospital overnight to be safe. He didn't have anything to do with my case, but he was adamant and seemed sincerely worried.

It was a good thing that I stayed because my condition quickly worsened and they were able to run more tests before finally realizing that my appendix had burst. They operated on me right away and saved me just in time. I owe my life to that surgeon who stopped us from going home that day. If he had been one second late, he would've missed us completely and my life would have ceased to exist. All that I am now rested on that pivotal moment and I am forever grateful to him for stepping in when he did. That is why several weeks later, after I was healed, my family and I went back to the hospital with a big present to give him. We wrapped up the gift really nicely and wrote a card. But the weirdest thing was, when we got to the hospital, no one knew who this surgeon was. No one knew who we were speaking of even though we asked for him by name and described his appearance. To them, there was no such person that existed. Puzzled and dumb-founded, we went home with the present still in hand. To this day, we still have not figured out who this mysterious benefactor is.

Personally, I believe he is an angel who came in and helped during a dire situation. Ever since that fateful day, I have become fond of prayer and have grown more and more convinced that something else is at work in the universe. Although it is not my expertise to produce scientific proof or evidence about the efficacy of prayer, my life experiences have shown me not to doubt its power. I actively encourage you to pray during your times of trouble and in your daily life as well. My firm belief is that you will always receive guidance in some form. And who knows, you may just receive your own miracle.

24

Puffy Eyes

When I was in high school, I ditched school a lot. There came a point where I was ditching school probably two or three times a week. It became a habit. I would forge letters from my parents and casually bring them to the office before walking home. One day, despite my carefulness, my mom was notified that I wasn't at school. Heartbroken and distressed, my mom promptly left work and came straight home.

When she walked through the door and I was completely caught unawares, I knew I was in *deep* trouble. My mom looked like she had been crying on the way home. She was a mixture of extreme anger and sadness.

"Why aren't you at school?!" she started. She was on the brink of going hysterical and I was still trying to gather myself from the shock of her being home.

"Why aren't you at school?" she asked again. I became a little teary-eyed and emotional as I braced myself to reveal the honest truth. Lowering my eyes, I told her in a soft voice, "Because I feel ugly." That caught my mom's attention and for a brief moment, her anger seemed to lift. "What do you mean you feel ugly?" she prodded.

"My puffy eyes, I hate my puffy eyes," I continued. "I feel so ugly because of them. It makes me not want to be at school."

My mom's tense posture suddenly relaxed and she no longer seemed angry at all, but rather kind of sad. Perhaps those words sounded all too familiar to her. My mom had also grown up constantly thinking she was ugly. She suffered heavily from low self-esteem and often fixated on parts of herself that she didn't like. She never felt good enough compared to her sister and felt wounded whenever people made comments about the two of them. For much of her life, she didn't think very highly of herself at all.

Without saying another word, my mom retreated upstairs and I instinctively knew she was no longer mad. My honest revelation seemed to sadden her in an entirely different way.

Looking back, I'm so grateful that my mom gave me a chance to explain myself before blowing up. Things looked bad; *really* bad. But before delivering an instant punishment, she took the time to understand what happened first and ended up not being too harsh on me. That event encouraged me greatly and also helped me become more understanding in my marriage. When something looked bad on the outside, I would try to hold off on the blame and investigate what happened first. A lot of times, things just turned out to be a misunderstanding or there was a perfectly good reason for what happened. I've learned that taking a pause and calmly giving the other person the benefit of the doubt is a very kind thing to do. Allow them a chance to explain and most likely, there will not even be a real cause for anger in the first place.

25

Pants

When I was a teenager, I was very particular about the clothes I wore. I always wanted to keep up with the latest trends at school so that I could fit in with everyone. The worst possible thing that could happen in my eyes was to stand out in a bad way and become a source of mockery. Sometimes, the way I dressed didn't agree with my parents. One Saturday morning, I went to attend a religious event near my house. My mom was there already and when she saw me, she pulled me aside right away. She didn't like the way I wore my pants. She wanted me to fix them right then and there because they were not appropriate in her eyes. I refused and protested. "Why should I?" I retorted. I wanted her to leave me alone. We started bickering and eventually got into a full-fledged fight. We parted ways, both fuming. I later learned that she went to vent to a fellow practitioner who was there that day. He listened to her plight and then asked her a simple question at the end: "Are a pair of pants more important than your relationship with your daughter?" The words struck my mom on her head like a hammer and she realized how silly it all was. No, it was not worth it to fight over a simple pair of pants. That moment became the turning point of our negative interaction that day and soon after, she calmly approached me, relaying what that man had said to her.

Although those words were spoken to her, I found that they were meant for me too. Did I really have to insist on wearing my pants like that if it bothered my mom so much? Couldn't I just humor her and do what she wanted for once? They were just pants after all. But my mother… well, she's my mother. Which is more important?

I never forgot this lesson and often remind myself of it still when I'm arguing with my husband. I'll stop and ask myself, "Wait, Shani. What is more important: this thing we're fighting about? Or my husband?" More often than not, the thing we're fighting about is trivial and not worthy of my anger. The next time you're unhappy with your spouse, just keep this in mind—whatever you're fighting about, you're giving it more importance than your relationship. Is it worth it?

26

The Coin

One of the things that drew me to my husband when we were dating was how stable and responsible he seemed. He was like a rock that I could rely on. Since I was the baby of my family growing up, I enjoyed being around someone who was so mature and always ready to take care of me.

After we got married, however, his serious and responsible nature turned into one of the things I disliked most about him. He became *too* serious and *too* responsible for my taste, often making the air feel tense in our house. He worried about everything and often wanted things done that I thought were unnecessary. I wished he would just lighten up and be more carefree. As an aspiring nun, I didn't want to be overcome with negative feelings towards my husband in this regard, but I was having trouble understanding him.

One day, after talking with a friend, though, I finally understood what it was like to be in my husband's shoes. My friend was, without knowing, stuck in my husband's position and she was complaining about her carefree husband not contributing enough to the household. She was venting all her troubles to me and through it all, I was able to gain insight into my husband's stance.

All the things my husband is able to provide for my family and me—including allowing me to be a stay-at-home-mom—comes at a tremendous cost: a whole lot of *pressure*. It is pressure that I wouldn't know about because I've always been sheltered my whole life. My carefree nature always came at the expense of others. And for the first time, I realized how unfair I was being for blaming my husband for how he was. It's true that sometimes he worries a lot and is too serious, but it's

41

also because of those traits that I'm able to benefit so much. Everything is taken care of for me and I have nothing to worry about in life, hence my carefree nature. He takes all the pressure off of me and burdens himself with it instead.

If I like how my husband is responsible and reliable, then I must also accept the fact that sometimes he can be uptight and strict. It's all part of the same coin. The good often comes with the bad and we must accept that. The trick is to see the relationship between the two and then focus on the good. That way, we can be reminded of what we love about our spouse and what drew us to them in the first place while showing gratitude for the kindness that they show.

27

The Ultimatum

Several years into dating James, I became increasingly bothered by five of his habits which included drinking and smoking among other things. I wanted him to quit these unhealthy habits and become completely "clean" like me. I started getting frustrated when he showed minimal to no signs of improving. One day, at the height of my frustration, I typed out an ultimatum and delivered it to his door- step. In a nice way, I basically said, "Please quit these habits or I'm breaking up with you." His reaction surprised me. He was mad! I wasn't expecting him to be mad because I thought I wrote the letter in a nice tone and tried to be very careful with his feelings. Besides, couldn't he see that it was all for his own good?

What I failed to see was that I was not coming from a place of understanding or compassion. Rather, I was coming from a place of judgement and rejection. I was essentially saying, "I don't love these parts of you, so get rid of them. *Then* I'll love you." Although I told myself it was all for his own benefit, the truth was, it had become all about my own benefit. I wanted him to change immediately for me, on my timetable. Maybe I was worried about how it made others look at me or how his habits would affect my life. It was very selfish thinking and revolved completely around me.

Not only that, but by wanting him to change, I was essentially declaring that I was better than him. I was placing myself above him and asking him to be more like me. Without knowing, I was pitting myself against him and creating an air of hostility and judgement which is not conducive for positive change.

It would be better, I later realized, if I learned to accept and love my husband whole-heartedly, *just as he is*. I should not try to change him at all. And if I'm truly concerned about his well-being, I should lead by example. I should demonstrate, by my own life and story, the vibrancy, health and love I wish for him. I would have a much better chance of influencing him for the better by living my life well and by regarding him with sincere love and acceptance. The problem was not in my husband, but instead, in my need to change him. In the end, I found that my only job is to embrace the man before me and to love him just the way he is.

28

Heaven

I would love to tell you that my honeymoon in Hawaii was absolutely perfect and flawless in every way. But the truth is, my husband and I were bickering before the plane even landed. (It was over something like who could see out the window). Perhaps we were both worn out from all the wedding planning that had led up to the honeymoon and were both running short on patience.

Either way, stepping foot onto "paradise" in my foul mood made me feel like I was anywhere but in paradise. The gorgeous tropical views were wasted on my anger and feelings of irritation. It didn't matter that I was in one of the most beautiful destinations on Earth, I was upset. And no amount of trees or sand could make me feel better.

People often think that heaven is a place you go to where you'll automatically be happy because of your surroundings. But from what I've observed, our surroundings have less to say about our happiness than our minds do. Just because you're in a beautiful place does not necessarily guarantee happiness because you may be disturbed over something in your mind and that would just ruin everything. Therefore, I do believe that heaven is a state of mind rather than a physical or material place.

I'm glad to say that my husband and I were able to get over our petty argument quite quickly and were able to go on to have a great time in Hawaii. But being unhappy in paradise taught me a huge lesson on how important our minds are in deciding our well-being.

It doesn't matter where you are, it's your mind that decides whether you're in heaven or hell. If you harbor the correct mindset and attitude, I believe you can be happy even in a jail cell. The mind is free and can never be trapped, unless trapped by your own limited thinking. That is the beauty of possessing such a powerful tool of being able to think. By simply training your mind, you can always reside in a place of bliss and have control over your own happiness. We just have to work on altering our thoughts and if we are successful, *paradise can be anywhere.*

29

Unwanted Tasks

I grew up in a family that didn't like to cook much. Cooking was often regarded as a tedious chore. We ate simply and in later years, ate mostly the same things. Perhaps this shaped my relationship with food and I didn't care much for pursuing delicious things. In college, when I was living away from my family, I preferred eating a bowl of cereal out of convenience than cooking a meal from scratch for enjoyment. I often scarfed down meals in a hurry not even remembering what I ate. Simply put, eating was not a big priority for me. It seemed like such a waste of time in the course of a busy day.

My husband couldn't be more opposite of me. He *loves* food. He loves eating and cooking and makes the most delicious meals mixing spices, sauces and ingredients I've never even heard of. He places a great amount of importance on food and finds great enjoyment in it.

One time, James and I took my sister to a vegetarian restaurant by the beach. James ordered a burger and ended up not liking it (to put it nicely). My sister commented later that James looked positively *offended* to be served such an awful thing. I smiled to myself, knowing, "Yup! That's my husband." He takes food very seriously.

Given this and the impending situation at home where I would soon become head chef, I had quite a bit of pressure on my shoulders. When it came time, I dreaded the task of cooking every day and felt so much anxiety over the chore because I didn't have any interest or experience in the area. Cooking would always be a source of stress for me.

One day, however, I realized that cooking was never going away and as my guru had taught me, I had better change my relationship with it. Otherwise, I would suffer indefinitely. I had to change my opinion about this task somehow. First, I started by listing out all the pros and cons. That was pretty easy; the biggest pro for me was that it would save my husband stress from having to deal with more chores after work. That reason alone definitely outweighed all the cons and naturally helped me to move forward a little bit. Next, I did something I hadn't done before. I broke down the huge task of cooking into little steps that I could actually take. I realized that I don't have to be a master chef overnight. That's too overwhelming for a beginner. Instead, I just need to start out small and learn how to cook basic things, like, an egg for example. I collected some recipes online and even saved some cooking videos which ended up being tremendously helpful later on. With practice, I saw that cooking was just a matter of following step-by-step instructions and anyone could do that.

After I got the ball rolling, I found that cooking wasn't so hard after all. It even reminded me of doing arts and crafts sometimes, which I love. I get to dice, chop and get my hands dirty while making something artistic. The hardest part was actually overcoming the mental block I had developed since childhood.

When my husband liked something I cooked, I felt so elated and gratified. It pushed me forward to try more recipes and to experiment with more different foods. It flushed me with happiness knowing that I was cooking for my family and that it was healthy. As things progressed,

I also started developing an affinity for farmer's markets where I could find fresh, colorful produce in an outdoor, and relaxing environment. The sight of fresh veggies and fruits would entice my senses. I really delved into the richness of life and explored this new amazing world. I cooked and cooked and it got easier and easier. Isn't that the case with all things though? It only takes a fresh perspective and some repetition, then all things are made easy. Being married often puts us in a position where we have to do things we don't like. But make it a point to conquer the challenge and it will never be a cause of frustration for you again.

Tips:
To tackle an undesirable chore,
- First list out the pros and cons
- Then break down the task into little chunks
- Encourage yourself
- Relate it to something you enjoy
- Lastly, see the beauty in what you're doing

30

True Compassion

During my training to become a nun, I learned that there are different levels of compassion. The easier level involves showing compassion to those who are kind to us or to those who are innocent and suffering from a great tragedy. Feelings of sorrow and love spring easily from our hearts as we imagine their pain. The more advanced and less discussed level of compassion involves showing compassion to those who *hurt* us. It requires some training of the mind and intentional shaping of thought. However, if you are skillful enough to achieve it, you will have truly understood the essence of compassion. Otherwise, you are merely being a slave to your feelings. Being able to show kindness to those who hurt you is beneficial in marriage as well because there are plenty of opportunities to get hurt when two people interact so often with one another.

While practicing compassion, I found a quote from an unknown source that has helped the process go along more easily. It goes: "*People need love the most when they deserve it the least.*" I have found this statement to bear much truth after careful observation throughout the years. It is actually those who act out in the most unlikable ways who are in the greatest need for care and attention. This ideology goes against all of our natural tendencies though. In the face of someone who hurts us, our first instinct is to recoil or to react negatively. But to exhibit extra kindness and care? It seems like madness. "They don't deserve it!" we might think. However, being kind to the enemy is the true test of compassion. It is what will make you stand out against the ordinary.

This concept is easier to understand when looking at children. Oftentimes, when a child comes from a broken family or has suffered a terrible trauma growing up, they are more likely to exhibit behavioral problems. It is a manifestation of their deep pain, which they do not know how to positively eliminate. Their defiance or withdrawal stems from an aspect of themselves that is broken and needs tending to. These children actually need love the most despite them "deserving it the least."

In the same way, when my husband is acting really difficult or mean, I can automatically surmise that he is going through some inner turmoil and needs extra care at the moment. I have to untangle myself from the mar of emotions that surge onto the shore of my mind and allow logic to form a conclusion about the situation. I need to remove myself from how things appear and delve deeper into the reasoning behind his behavior. It is not personal; he is simply ailing. It is an opportunity to put his needs above my own and to answer his indirect cry for help. Of course this practice can be excruciatingly difficult, but it is absolutely achievable and worth striving for.

31

The Neighbor

I was walking my dog, Hercules, around my parent's neighborhood one afternoon. He stopped at a house to pee and I waited for him, like any other time.

Suddenly, a loud, menacing voice came booming from behind the screen door of the house we were at. It was a man's voice, snarling and cussing. He was furious and yelling a slur of words. He had been watching us and was now accusing my dog of pooping on his lawn. Clearly, that was not the truth. My dog was simply urinating. But being too startled to defend myself, I just instinctively apologized and hurried along, still hearing his loud voice yelling behind me.

Later, I thought about what had happened and strangely, I was not the least bit upset. Rather, I was reflecting on how the man had unleashed so much fury over such a small matter. From my collective experiences, I knew that the man was probably not a happy person especially if he could react in such an explosive way towards a perfect stranger. There must be a lot of things bothering him already. When I thought about it further, his house looked like a pitiful mess from the outside—peeling paint, overgrown weeds and a junk boat parked on the driveway. If his house was a reflection of his mind, then he was not doing very well at all. My heart felt for him then and I empathized with his situation. A quote by Mark Twain also came to mind at this time. "Let us live so that when we come to die, even the undertaker will be sorry." Those words were motivation for me to become a vessel of kindness even though the man had been mean to me. I wanted to soften his heart. That's when I decided to do something most people would find strange. I sat down at my desk and wrote him the friendliest and sincerest card that I could muster (I opted to leave out any personal information for safety reasons). I apologized for having offended him earlier in any way and for causing such an inconvenience. I wished him well and even enclosed a five-dollar gift card which I had found in my wallet. I explained it wasn't much but I hope he'd accept it as a token of my sincere sentiments.

Sealing up my letter, I was beginning to feel tickled just thinking about what his reaction might be. I only wished I could be there in person to witness it. At the very least, it would leave him confused.

What I've learned is that it doesn't take any restraint or self-discipline to unleash anger and take revenge on an enemy. But to act with control and kindness under offensive circumstances? That is a true feat. Instead of retaliating, act in a way that catches the person off guard. Meet hatred with kindness and watch their bewilderment unfold. What usually follows is self-reflection and regret upon their own behavior. If you ever find yourself in an offensive circumstance with your spouse (which is likely to happen over the course of one's marriage) try reacting with utter kindness and most likely, you will move something deeply in their heart, leaving a memorable impression.

32

Criminal

After being introduced to the concept of compassion, I wanted to be an overachiever and master the most difficult level. I wanted to practice loving the most fearsome and most frightening, unlovable people on earth. That's why, when I was at a bookstore, one specific book caught my eye. It was a book detailing the lives of the most terrifying serial killers in America. I was scared to read it but also felt curious about the backgrounds of these people. I ended up buying the book to do my own personal research.

I never did finish reading the book completely, I was too afraid and disturbed by some of the things they did. But there was one important lesson I gathered through reading many of those biographies. Those hardened killers, those helplessly lost souls, had all come from a broken childhood, grew up in a toxic environment or had strong emotional pains that were never dealt with properly. It was the same story, case after case. They were ailing in some way and their terrifying behavior was emanating from that pain. After this discovery, it was not so hard to exercise a little compassion on them. I had grown up in a very wholesome and protective environment, with my family intact. I felt loved and surrounded by supportive people growing up and never felt the need to go out and do outrageous, harmful things. But many of those people I read about did not have such accommodating lives. They were often abused and put through the ringer, completely devoid of a nurturing environment. I believe the terrible choices they made were stemmed, in some way, from the hurt in their lives.

This thought humbled me, for I wondered: If I were put under conditions like theirs, *would I turn out a criminal myself?*

Understanding the lives of those who have become lost has helped me understand my husband more as well. When he acts in a way that doesn't appeal to me or even hurts my feelings, I am more inclined to view the situation differently because I know that he doesn't necessarily mean to give me pain. That's just part of his limitations as a person. Wrongful behavior is always a sign that someone is not whole in some way. If someone is whole and healthy and loving, then they would never hurt others. They would only bring joy and comfort.

33

Dirty Socks

I once heard a true story about a woman who would always nag at her husband to un-bunch his dirty socks before throwing them into the laundry basket. For years, she nagged at him about this and for years, he kept to his same old habits. Although it was just a small thing, it annoyed her to no end because he simply ignored her requests. One day however, the woman found her husband's socks neatly un-bunched in the laundry basket. She could scarcely believe her eyes. He had listened for once! She hurriedly rushed to her husband and showered him with praise.

"You helped me out this time and did what I asked! It makes my life so much easier," she gushed. She made sure to really lather on the praise and he beamed like a little child, holding a lollipop. From that time on, he made it a point to un-bunch his socks every time.

It's amazing what a little praise can do. It is such a powerful motivator. The nuns understand this and often use praise to guide people along the righteous path in an encouraging way. Most people use praise to uplift little children and innocent pets who are learning their way through the early stages of life. But how quickly this method is abandoned once adults are in the picture or when two married people are concerned. Nagging often takes the place of praise and negative sentiments quickly fill the home while two vastly different people with vastly different habits must learn to coexist. This is very sad because praise, on the other hand, can be so effective and inspiring. It can bring out the shiniest parts of someone and fill the home with positivity.

I remember experiencing the effects of praise myself one time. I had just gotten married and felt a bit overwhelmed with how neat and clean my new house was expected to be. I grew up in a family of "free spirits" who didn't mind a little dust or clutter here and there. But now, in this new setting, I was expected to maintain the upkeep of the spotless place. With two stories of hardwood floors and four bedrooms, I felt overwhelmed with the household chores. It seemed like I could never get the place clean enough for some people's standards.

Then one day, my husband's aunt came to visit from Taiwan. When she walked in, she looked around with delighted eyes and said, "Wow Shani, you've made this place so clean! You're so good at making things neat." As she spoke, I felt my face blooming like a flower in the warm sun. I was completely elated. I felt like I could clean the house endlessly for her just to please her further.

From that instance, I understood firsthand the power of praise and why the nuns actively utilize this method. I felt how strongly I wanted to change for my husband's aunt simply because she had recognized my efforts and had given me encouragement for the journey. If you want someone to change or to do a certain thing, praise them. Praise them often and sincerely and watch them transform before your very eyes.

34

Charging Batteries

For a big part of my life, I never allowed myself the enjoyment of having friends in the way that the world did. I sought out people who I instinctively felt were lonely, filled with pain or unlovable to others, not people whom I genuinely enjoyed being around. I felt like it was a waste of time to make friends with people who were thriving and surrounded by love because they were happy already. My focus was always on those in need.

As a result, socializing always became an act of exertion on my part. I was always giving myself away. It wasn't always an enjoyable experience for me. In fact, it mostly felt like a chore because I didn't truly enjoy the presence of my friends, I just enjoyed feeling like I was needed and making a difference.

Over time, the act of giving and giving wore me out. My patience eventually grew thin because I did not have healthy friends to balance out this lifestyle I had taken upon myself. I did not have methods of recharging my mental state once I was tired. Everything that exerts energy needs to be recharged, just like our phones and appliances. When they run out of battery, we need to plug them into a source to recharge them. If not, the object would no longer work. That's what happened to me. I eventually couldn't handle all those friends I was trying to "help."

My lifestyle wasn't healthy because I wasn't taking care of myself. I felt that I had an obligation only to serve and not to have fun. It was selfish to do anything for my own benefit. But later, I learned a new concept from the temple. How can you take care of others if you, yourself, are drowning? You are not giving your best gift when you are depleted and run down. *You must take care of yourself first before you can take care of others.* If you really see things in this light, then you'll find that taking care of yourself first is one of the biggest steps you can take towards being compassionate. You are making yourself whole to give others a loving and radiant version of yourself. That's when I found that making friends for my own enjoyment is not selfish but is actually necessary for my well-being in the long run.

This is equally relevant in my marriage because I find that when I'm rested, healthy and happy, I am a better partner to my husband. When I take care of myself, I prevent a lot of arguments from taking place because I feel physically well and have a lot of patience to spare.

Taking care of yourself is the best preventative measure you can take against unhappiness in your marriage. So please, nourish your body. Nourish your mind. Nourish your spirit. Indulge in the things that bring you joy. Do it for yourself and for those you love.

35

Surprises

One Friday night at around 11:00 p.m., James asked me, "Are you tired?"

I replied no.

"Will you go somewhere with me real fast?" he continued.

I thought that was weird, but I said okay. He told me to put on something warm. Then, we got into my car and he started driving. He made me close my eyes and promise not to open them until we reached our destination. We got on the freeway ramp (I could tell that much) but I really didn't have a clue where we were going. It seemed like we were on the freeway for a long time before we exited and finally arrived somewhere.

Turns out, James had carefully planned an outing for us while he was at work. He knew exactly what he was doing. When the car parked, he finally allowed me to open my eyes. I sat up and looked around. I was confused at first because it was dark and we were surrounded by other cars. But when a giant screen flickered on to life in front of us, I knew where we were. We were at a drive-in movie theater. He reached into the backseat and pulled out a pan of popcorn which he had pre-popped at home. He also brought other snacks—licorice to help with my cold, chips and a warm ginger drink in a thermos—plus a pillow and blanket. I was floored. It was exciting and unexpected especially since we had been staying home every weekend before that night. I was quite moved and appreciated how even after being together for so long, he still made efforts to plan surprises.

He taught me that consideration towards your spouse doesn't have to end when things get comfortable. Being together with someone year after year also does not have to equate to boring and uninspired. It reminded me of life in the temple and how much of it is routine. Much of the same things are done every day at the same times. It could easily get boring and dull. But it's up to each practitioner to derive new inspiration and meaning from the normal events that happen. How does one see everything with fresh eyes? For my husband and me, much of what happens in our lives is routine as well. But his creativity reminded me of all the exciting adventures that are waiting for us out there if we look at the world with a new outlook. Don't let those opportunities go to waste. Go out there and seek the world. Experience all that life has to offer, together.

My husband's thoughtfulness prompted me to start plotting a surprise of my own which filled me with excitement. I found that life is really fun when lived this way; when constantly thinking over how to make the other person happy. It really breathes new life into the relationship and promotes romantic sentiments as there is no sweeter display of love than this.

36

Cuteness

Everybody is cute in their own way. Yes, *everybody*. It may be hard to see where someone is cute, but as my guru liked to say, "Just because you can't see something doesn't mean it's not there. We simply lack the eyes to see it."

When we find a thing to be cute, we are, in essence, discovering its innocence and purity. It is easy to love the things that are innocent and pure to us. That is why it is so important to dig out those qualities in our spouse that we find cute. It helps to soften our hearts toward them and to love them more.

My husband probably wouldn't appreciate being called "cute." He'd probably prefer "tough," "strong," or "masculine." But still, I see cuteness in him shine through. For example, I find it cute how he delicately sprinkles salt into soup. It always makes me smile. He's such a big guy with big hands. But when he's cooking, he's as gentle as ever, treating the spice bottles like his little babies. He puts so much care into his cooking.

When he pours liquid into a tiny bottle, he always sticks out his chubby little pinky finger. His face looks so serious, but his pinky sticking straight up in the air just looks so funny to me. Or when he wraps our baby's diaper, he always has to bundle it up into a tight, little perfect tamale. It's perfect every time. Seeing the diaper always makes me laugh because it shows his obsessive need to reach perfection in all that he does. I find that cute.

Discover what it is about your spouse that *you* find cute. Constantly search for his innocence and let it strengthen your love towards him. Find the ways in which he is adorable to you and watch your heart grow fonder of him every day.

37

Two Words

As a spiritual warrior, I've found that one of the most difficult practices ever (*ever*) is to say sorry first. Although "I'm sorry" are just two words, they can seem impossibly heavy to say, like two-ton boulders sitting on the tongue. The words may form inside the mouth but getting them out is a different story.

Perhaps saying sorry is especially hard when you feel like you are 100% correct or when you feel you've been wronged. "Why should I?" is usually the first thought that comes to mind. Pride is such a heavy thing to lift. So often, we'd rather hold onto our pride and watch a relationship disintegrate than to be the first ones to make amends. That is why only a masterful practitioner can overcome their ego and apologize first. As my teacher taught, a practitioner has the responsibility of saying sorry first because they are practicing the way of virtue. Some might think apologizing is for the weak, but the wise know better. It is actually the courageous and strong who can step down from their pedestals to initiate peace.

Therefore, if you are able to approach one who has done you wrong and forgive them, that is a sign of true maturity. You did something difficult and you should be proud of yourself.

It should be noted that apologies are best if they are sincere and if no defensive comments are made afterward. No one likes to hear an apology that is quickly followed by a "but" and a reiteration of why the person was mad in the first place. That defeats the whole purpose of an apology. Just tell them you're sorry and let that be the end of the sentence. I always notice that my husband becomes more affectionate after I've spared him the hardship of apologizing first. He knows in his heart that I've shown him a great kindness.

38

Grumpiness

Girls usually get a bad rep for being moody. But from my experience, guys can be just as moody if not more so.

One of the more challenging aspects of my marriage was dealing with my husband's frequent grumpiness. He got grumpy a lot and it would affect me because I'm so sensitive to other people's moods. I used to take it really personally and feel hurt whenever he expressed any unhappiness towards me. But I have since learned that his grumpiness stems from a source outside of myself and that there is no need for me to feel hurt.

To better illustrate what I mean, let's take a look at little children. When children are cranky and grumpy, parents instinctively know that their little ones are tired and need a nap. The moodiness is caused by their physical feelings of discomfort. Parents put their children to sleep and soon enough, the littles ones wake up refreshed and happy again.

Adults operate in very similar ways. (Adults and children actually have much more in common than we realize). When adults are grumpy, most likely they are experiencing physical or mental discomfort. Once those discomforts are dealt with, the moodiness usually goes away.

When I thought about it, my husband became much grumpier after our baby was born. Single-handedly, he had to support three people and the burden was quite great. It made sense that his mood suffered a lot because of this dramatic change. He was constantly tired and under tremendous pressure. He even started growing bald spots on his head from stress and developing dark circles under his eyes from lack of sleep. His grumpiness was a manifestation of his physical *and* mental discomforts.

When seen in this light, I no longer took my husband's outbursts to heart. I recognized that he needed either more rest, more ways to de-stress, or simply more attention. What he *didn't* need was for me to react dramatically to his behavior and cause more difficulties.

If you can think in such a way, a way that considers the other person's situation, you can really help others in their times of suffering just as nuns strive to do. Don't just look at the effect that is manifesting before you. Look for the cause and always try your best to act with kindness.

39

Daily Discipline

pride myself in not getting mad that often and, surprisingly, I've found that when I *do* get mad, it carries more weight. My husband seems to become anxious and uncomfortable if I'm unhappy or acting coldly towards him. Thus, I've learned that practicing restraint on a normal basis has its benefits. On the other hand, if someone is always getting upset or picking fights, then it starts to become tiresome and repetitive for the people around them. Others eventually become desensitized and tune out that unpleasant voice.

I knew a couple once. The guy was often debating and arguing over every little thing. He liked to pick fights and challenge others' notions, even if he firmly believed in those same notions himself. On the other hand, his wife was a gentle, sweet-tempered woman who didn't speak much and seemed rather shy.

On one occasion, I was with this couple and the guy was chatting on as usual. He made a rather unpleasant remark at one point and it didn't sit well with his wife. For the first time, I saw the wife flash an unpleasant look at her husband and he immediately went quiet. In fact, throughout the rest of the evening, he seemed rather bothered that his wife was unhappy and made obvious attempts to win back her affections. I had never seen him so accommodating before. All it took was one look from her to send him into a panic. Now *that* is sheer power! But I imagine it took a lot of self-restraint and effort for her to avoid getting mad at every turn in the past. Her self-discipline allowed her to achieve this gentle grace in the current moment.

What I saw through her example just reinforced what I had already come to believe: we should not fight for every little battle. We must pick and choose the ones that are truly important to us. The less fights we pick, the more weight they hold.

40

The White Plate

It was the weekend and James and I were eating at a new restaurant. We were seated in a private corner at the back of the room, enjoying the peace and quiet to ourselves. Suddenly, the white-haired owner appeared at the front of the restaurant and started passing out little white plates of free samples to everyone. Our mouths started watering as we watched him move from table to table. He went around the room and everyone got their plates. Everyone except for us. Then the owner disappeared and didn't come back. Our salivating mouths were disappointed as we realized he had missed our table. It seemed unfair that everyone got something except for us. Even though it was just a little thing, it put a damper on our meal because, let's face it. No one likes to feel left out.

On our way out, my eyes lit up because I found a small table with the same white plates sitting on top. I took a closer look to see what we had missed earlier and I was surprised. They were filled with browning pieces of old fruit. Oh my. I didn't want to eat that and actually felt glad that the owner had missed our table. How silly were we to have almost let that unappealing thing ruin our meal? We wanted so badly to have what others had that it took our focus off of what we had already and left a bitter taste in our mouths.

This analogy reminds me of how I sometimes wish I could trade my husband in for another, especially during those times when things aren't going so well. I entertain thoughts like, "Oh, wouldn't it be nice if

I was with someone more easy going and mellow?" One time, I envied a friend whose husband was known to be very patient. He had such a calm personality and rarely got mad. But several months later, I found out that this husband was also very stingy. I decided I'd rather have my grump of a husband than a penny-pincher. That's when I realized that there is no one perfect in every way. If I married someone else, they would have other traits that I *don't* desire, which my current husband already has. The search for perfection becomes futile. There are always good and bad factors to every single person.

Instead of always looking outwards and seeing what other people have, I realized I should direct my gaze right in front of me and wholeheartedly appreciate what I have *right now*. Everything I have can be worked with and can be made desirable, depending on how I look at it. If I got my wish and my husband became just like me, then a lot of things would never get done. I'm playful, he's more serious. He's the taskmaster, I'm the one that makes sure he relaxes. If we both relaxed all the time, then nothing would get done. The truth is, there's a reason why I chose him as my husband and why we were both attracted to each other in the first place. We both have something the other needs.

If I never feel grateful for anything I have, then that is akin to a beggar who is always thirsting and never satisfied. I don't want to be forever in pursuit of an elusive object only to come up with nothing because of my unending desire for more. That would be a waste of a life. But if, instead, I can become content with what I have, then I will be rich, enjoying all that is given to me. The fullness of life will be upon me, simply with a grateful heart. Stop pursuing what others have and just be content with your lot. Whatever you have can be worked with. Whatever you have can be good if you allow yourself to see it.

41

Sex

The word sex is not really part of a nun's vocabulary. In fact, the words nun and sex almost seem like opposites to me. Needless to say, having sex went against my training as a nun. Women and men were strictly separated in temples and for my particular sect, were not even allowed to so much as look at each other. Having submerged myself in this pure environment for so long, I initially thought it was unholy to have sex. I was "making myself dirty." But I soon realized that rules which apply in one area do not necessarily apply in another. It's all about the context of the situation. Being in a marriage makes *everything* different. You have to account for the other person's feelings and needs, not just your own. That's the whole point about marriage actually. You can't just do whatever you, yourself, feel like because you are now part of a team. Your actions affect someone else directly. You always have to think about how your partner feels. That is what it means to act from love and to be considerate.

There have been times where I have witnessed my husband being really stressed out or tense. But after having sex, he always seemed to relax and loosen up. It seemed to release a lot of frustrations and negativity that had built up inside him. I don't understand it but I've seen the physical benefits it gives him and the immediate sense of relief it brings. I often keep that in mind when I notice he's had a really bad day, looks completely stressed out, or has gone for a period of time without it. Most likely, he could use a little attention.

One time, James was acting unreasonably upset over something small. He was getting so tangled up in anger and nothing could convince him to let it go. I found that any talking I did was not working and so I decided to try "taking care of him." Afterwards, I asked him how he felt about the situation he had been complaining about and he replied, "Oh that? It's not a big deal at all." Then, he rolled over in bed and curled up like a giant koala. He was completely relaxed and content.

I was perplexed but intrigued. Later on, I found that James could be having the worst day of his life and still, sex will fix it. No matter how angry or upset he appears to be, it can always dissolve his frustrations; he'll emerge from it a docile little baby. It's kind of nice to discover how my husband has a secret reset button. It makes things really easy sometimes.

In the end, my views toward sex are very simple. I don't need to view it as a dirty or shameful act. It's a normal part of marriage. Also, I tell myself to keep his feelings in mind as much as possible. Although I may not always be in the mood, I know that sex can act as a stress-reliever for him and that men are biologically built differently. Their needs may differ from those of women. I try to have consideration for his requests and to show kindness in this regard as I would in all other areas.

42

The Least Harmful Method

One day, I got tickets to a religious concert and I wanted James to go with me. It was an event that really interested me. It would've meant a lot to me if we could attend the concert together. I brought it up to him, making sure to catch him at a good time. But to my disappointment he immediately replied, "*No.*"

"Please?" I asked. "No."

No matter how much I begged for the rest of the evening, he would not comply and insisted that it was completely out of the question. "I'm not going to no religious thing!" he would say. It was difficult to change his mind. I could have gotten frustrated and I could have argued, "But I always agree to the things you want! I never ask anything of you! How could you be so unfair?"

However, I didn't go that route. Instead, I asked myself how a nun would act in this case and tried something different—a softer approach. I went up to him and stood right in front of him. Then, I looked up into his eyes with the saddest look I could muster.

"Pleeeeeeeease?" I asked, about to unload some tears if necessary. The softness in him kicked in and to my surprise, he finally agreed. "Fine," he replied softly. I was shocked at how painless this method was. I didn't have to fight him, I just had to activate the softness in him.

I would bet that your husband has a very soft spot for you too. After all, he married you, didn't he? Most likely, he would respond to an approach similar to the one I demonstrated.

The point of this technique is not to be manipulative or conniving. But rather, to use the least harmful method whenever possible to avoid unnecessary damage. If your husband responds to a pleading look, why resort to a gruesome war that could cause much more pain? Instead of gearing up for a fight right away, try being creative and use different methods to coax him. It may be easier than you think. Pay mind to his feelings if you can. Try to avoid being mean. Use your gifts as a woman and as his wife. Try the least harmful way to get what you want and you'll be tickled at how simple it is.

43

The Mirror

During an unhappy situation, it's easy to think about all the things the other person didn't do right and to keep dwelling on those thoughts over and over again. At home, I'll sometimes find myself thinking, "Look, there he goes, talking to me with that attitude again."

"See how impatient he is?" and so on and so forth. I would always want my husband to correct his behavior before I could be happy. But my guru eventually taught me a different way to approach things. Instead of pointing a finger outwards, we should pause and look into the situation more honestly. Can I ask myself, "Did I do everything right? Was there something *I* could've done better?" Most likely there was. Maybe I could've been more careful about the other person's feelings. Maybe I could've exercised more patience. The trick is to always direct the mirror inwards and to correct ourselves when we can. We can't control anything that happens on the outside, but we can control ourselves and what happens on the inside. My teacher raised an analogy in regards to this concept. Instead of covering the whole Earth with a layer of leather to protect our feet from the spiky rocks, it would be far more productive to simply put a layer of leather under our own feet. Then, we will be protected no matter where we go. That is another way of saying we should equip ourselves with all that we need to be content instead of depending on others to provide the perfect environment. Stepping up and taking responsibility for ourselves is the smartest way to gain freedom over unpleasant situations in our lives. A true practitioner works at improving his own faults; he always directs the mirror inwards and expects nothing of others.

44

Smile

It was a Sunday afternoon and I was in a rotten mood. I was at the supermarket, pushing my baby around in a cart and feeling utterly grumpy. I tried to talk positively to myself but nothing worked; I just couldn't shake off how I felt. Then, while we were at the check-out line, an elderly lady appeared out of nowhere to bag our groceries. She wore a huge childish grin on her face as she said hello and leaned in to play with my baby. She was so sweet and cheerful, talking and interacting with us so happily while bagging our things. I couldn't take my eyes off this lady's infectious smile as she spread her good cheer to all of us.

As we left, waving bye to this woman, I felt lighter and brighter. My mood had completely changed during our short exchange. I realized she had lit me up from within with her positive energy. She had unloaded my burden and transformed my day without even knowing it.

The truth is, living in this world can be hard sometimes. There are days that can be stressful and depressing. Although we may wear a smile on our faces in public, we may actually be holding in a lot of suffering inside. (Yes, we're all good at faking it!) That's why these little acts of kindness can go a long way.

That day at the market, I learned the power of a simple smile. A smile conveys warmth and friendliness. It draws people in and spreads cheerfulness. One smile from a stranger turned my whole day around. That lady showed me that I should smile more at people. There is nothing that makes a person more attractive or lovable.

Seeing the lady smile also reminded me that I should smile more to my husband even though we have been together for so long. Most likely, he needs my good cheer more than anyone because his stressful days are more visible to me than to other people. I am his companion in life. Who better to show him a happy face? Let's remember to show kindness to all those around us as we journey through this world together. Display your smiles proudly. Don't hold them back. Keep in mind that every intentional smile is an act of kindness and no act of kindness is ever wasted. It always makes a difference to someone, somehow.

45

Bangs

When my daughter was about 18 months old, her hair grew kind of long and it started covering her face. Her bangs needed to be trimmed but I was nervous to cut it. I didn't want to mess up. Luckily, James stepped up and said he could do it. He took a pair of scissors, pinched her bangs between his fingers, slid down the length of them and made a single cut all the way across. When he let go, I was horrified at what I saw. Her bangs were riding *very* high on her forehead. She looked like Jim Carrey from the movie, *Dumb and Dumber*.

"Shoot," my husband said. He knew he had messed up. "I shouldn't have cut her hair." He was obviously feeling bad. But after a couple days, we got over it and got used to her new hair. I even started thinking the whole ordeal was funny. When James and I were out with friends, I would tell them the story and everyone would laugh. One day, when we were in the presence of James' boss, someone asked about our daughter's hair and I happily launched into my story once again.

"What! James really cut her hair?" his boss asked. He found it so funny and couldn't stop laughing. He made a comment to his wife and they started laughing together. Everyone seemed amused and entertained. When we left, however, I discovered that James was upset. "Did you really have to do that?" he snapped. "How could you throw me under the bus in front of my boss? I already felt bad for what I did. Do you have to keep rubbing it in?"

I had no idea James was taking it that way. I thought he found the whole thing funny, just like I did. But actually, he was really embarrassed. From his perspective, I was making him look bad in front of the whole world and everyone was laughing at him. When I realized the impact my actions were having on him, I felt terrible for not being more sensitive. All I cared about was telling a funny story and getting some attention, but I did so at the expense of my husband.

From that time forth, I understood how important pride is to my husband (and to everyone for that matter) and that I should do my best to be careful with it. I try not to humiliate or shame him in front of other people as I know he can be very sensitive. Now, in the presence of others, I only strive to make him shine. When I make him look good in front of others, he definitely notices and appreciates it.

46

What Matters

A friend of mine named Jeremy Chou wrote a poignant piece which left a deep impression on me when I read it. He wrote:

> *My wife and I went to a beautiful memorial service this morning for a dear friend who just lost her husband to brain cancer. Out of all the stories the loved ones shared, it became apparent what was the most important memory*

everybody had of him. It wasn't about the material things. It wasn't about how big the house was, or how many toys he had bought for his three daughters. It was simply about the time he had spent with them. All the family trips they took together, all the family traditions, all the experiences they shared growing up with their wonderful father.

As parents, I think we all get trapped into thinking we always have to give our children the best. Let it be the best toys, best vacations, best of everything we can buy. However, at the end, the only thing that matter is the time you spent with your children.

Forget all the material things. Really, the best gift we can give our children is simply our time and attention.

I couldn't agree with Jeremy more. In this world where everything is so fleeting and fragile, our interaction with loved ones becomes ever so important.

Growing up in a large religious community made me accustomed to seeing death frequently starting at an early age. I was often present at services or helping to participate in rites for those who passed. We always think we have a lot of time, but actually we don't. Life is so short and unpredictable. When you truly understand the fact that everything has a time limit, you will approach everything differently. We're too used to thinking we'll always be around. "My husband will always be around. My family will always be around." But the truth of the matter is, we don't know. We don't know how much time we have left; how much time *anything* has left. We must cherish the precious moments we have with those we love and graciously set aside our ambitious pursuits for material things. Like Jeremy said, "Forget all material things." In the end, the only thing that truly matters is love.

47

Nothing Personal

One spring, I found myself walking happily around a charming city in a foreign country. The sun was out, the flowers were blooming and the atmosphere felt so relaxed. It was everything a beautiful day should be. And then suddenly, a tall white man walked by me and hissed, "Hey Chink, get off the road!"

I should've been mad. I should've been offended to the core. But somehow, nothing in my being felt like reacting negatively that day. I continued walking, unaffected. Sure, I may have been a little worried about my safety. I was small in stature and didn't want to get beat up on a street thousands of miles away from home. But aside from that, I didn't feel much anger or unhappiness at all.

Perhaps I failed to get mad because I recognized that his comment was a reflection of his own upbringing and collective life-experiences. Honestly, it had nothing to do with me. My presence just happened to trigger a part of who he was already. If I went to the market and a stranger struck up a nice conversation with me, their kindness would have nothing to do with me. It would just demonstrate that they were a nice person to begin with. I would not be able to take any credit for how they are. Their experiences in life are what landed them there. Whether people are nice or mean has nothing much to do with anything except themselves. Thus, I've learned not to take anything personally.

I used to get really hurt when my husband said some mean things to me. But over the years, I've familiarized myself with this concept. His behavior is triggered by his upbringing and a collection of other factors such as his mood. Maybe he was hungry or maybe he was subconsciously bothered by something. Whatever the case, how he behaves is a manifestation of various factors that were presented in his life and there is little I can do about it except not let it get to me. I know when I, myself, have had favorable circumstances fall onto my plate, I can burst into song and hug complete strangers on the street. Nothing can get me down. And when I'm upset, the sweetest-faced kitten can make me annoyed. It all depends on my mood or situation. It has nothing to do with the people I come into contact with. So just remember, everyone's actions stem from themselves and the things that are happening to them. Do yourself a favor and don't take anything personally.

48

OMAK

If there's only one thing you take away from this book, I hope it's this: OMAK (pronounced *oh-mak*). OMAK stands for Observe Merits and Appreciate Kindness. My late teacher taught me this phrase and throughout my marriage, it has proved to be most helpful.

Many years ago, my spiritual teacher became very ill. Sometimes, he stayed in bed for weeks at a time because he was too weak to get up. When visitors went to visit him, he was so happy because people thought of him when he wasn't feeling well. Therefore, on those days when I heard that no one went to visit him, I worried that he might feel sad and lonely. But the opposite was true. My teacher was once again so happy because, according to him, people were thoughtful enough to let him rest. Whatever situation came to him, he was content because he actively searched for merit and appreciated kindness. In this way, he was always happy because his mind was always in a positive place. Simply put, he was good at OMAK-ing.

As human beings, it's often our natural tendency to focus on the negative and to fixate on the things we don't like. This happens even more frequently in a marriage where two people are heavily involved in each other's lives and nothing is hidden from view. Faults rise to the surface with ease, and it becomes easy for each person to pick on the other.

"Why are you so messy?" one might complain. Or, "Why can't you just think before you do something?" "You're so lazy and selfish."

Resentment and bitterness quickly build in the home with each negative thought. I've found that the result of such destructive thinking can eventually lead to hate. It's scary how quickly love can turn into hate when one simply chooses to focus on the wrong things.

The teaching of OMAK is not to deny that there are faults, but rather, to just shed light on the merit that *does* exist. If we can simply shift our focus from the bad things to the good things that are present in every situation, then our hearts will be lighter, more appreciative, and more understanding. The result of this trend in thought is love and gratitude.

We are actually all very good at practicing OMAK when it comes to one particular situation: when it comes to viewing ourselves. We can overlook all of our bad qualities so long as we have one good quality to praise. We can always justify our behaviors or our traits because we are accustomed to holding ourselves in high esteem. If we can use that same standard of OMAK on others, then *everything* will be different. Our interactions will be drastically more positive and pleasant. Our hearts will be released of negativity and we will only see the best in others.

49

OMAK (Cont.)

Although the concept of OMAK seems simple enough, it is actually insanely hard to put into practice. When you feel mad at someone, you just want to get mad. The force is so strong. Stopping your anger is like stopping a moving train. Even after almost twenty years of devoted practice to OMAK, it is still very hard for me and I often fall short. The habit of picking out negativity is just too deeply ingrained in me. Perhaps a whole lifetime of practicing OMAK is still not enough to really get good at it.

One evening, James and I exchanged some heated words. Then I numbly left to go shower. I still remember while I was showering, my mind had not yet decided if it wanted to become angry or to OMAK. I could almost see a path splitting into two inside my head. Take the easy route and get mad? Or take the high road and observe his merits? My thoughts remained suspended in air and I wondered which way to tip the scale. It was difficult even to simply remain in that state of neutrality. In the end, I was able to succeed and push out the negative thoughts. Instead of focusing on what I was angry about, I started to ponder over nice things he had done for me that day.

"He went to the market after work to get me blueberries."

There, I had found something to start with. I wrapped my mind around that thought and tried to elaborate on it further.

"He was tired but still went to the market anyway. He cares."

Then my thoughts jumped to another place.

"He made me cabbage for dinner."

On and on this went, just like that—picking out all the nice things from the rubble of my mind. When I had really internalized the kind deeds he had done and meditated upon them one by one, I felt the anger slowly lift. Each thought eased the burden of my anger. You know you've succeeded when you start to think: "He's done so much for me; how can I stay mad?"

The idea is that you can't feel both anger and gratefulness at the same time. There is not enough room in our minds for both to exist simultaneously. We must let the good push out the bad. It's like, when you add white dots to a black canvas, and keep adding and adding, it eventually becomes white without you taking the black away. Likewise, if you keep OMAK-ing, those positive thoughts will overtake the bad without you having to take the bad away. It becomes effortless.

On another occasion, I was very frustrated with a lady. I felt that she was so unreasonable, mean, and unlikable—a downright bully! She was negative and condescending. I was consumed with anger towards her and the negative thoughts kept coming in relentless waves.

But, all of a sudden, a memory cut through my thoughts and silenced me; it was an act of kindness she had shown me once before. In it, she was persuading one of her friends to give me a lunch box because I needed one and her friend had plenty of them. When that lunch box finally made its way to me, I felt so grateful and touched by the sweet gesture.

Dwelling on this warm thought, my heart softened. It was a very nice memory that I had forgotten all about. Perhaps it was pushed back from all the resentment I now felt. But I didn't want to give in to the hate any longer. I knew about OMAK already. What kind of practitioner was I being? This woman had shown me kindness before and she was not all bad. She could actually be very generous.

As I hung on to her one act of kindness and recalled the friendliness she had demonstrated, I felt my feelings towards her change and from there, I knew I could proceed in a more loving manner. That is the power of focusing on merits rather than faults. In every situation, no matter how hopeless it may appear, there is *always* something positive to be found. The second I blame someone, I feel trapped. But when I OMAK, I create a path out and find peace.

50

My Nose

James' uncle made the trip from Northern California to our house in Southern California one day. He had brought his dog along for the long drive and had made it to our house in a single day. When they arrived, I greeted them as warmly as I could. While James explained some things to his uncle, I got down on my knees and introduced myself to the dog. I started petting him generously while talking to him like a baby. Suddenly, he lurched forward like a snake and bit down hard on my nose. I was in shock and felt a bit confused because it all happened so fast. Then, I felt a surge of immense pain gather on my nose and I quickly ran to the bathroom to check it out. I was horrified at what I saw. The dog had clearly bitten straight through my nose, leaving a hole in its place. Blood was starting to gush out and it was making one terrific mess.

Thinking back on this event, I find myself foolish for being so careless with the dog and for not observing the situation more closely. I was so eager to show care to the dog in my own way that I didn't even bother to observe what he really needed at the time. Perhaps he was tired from the long drive and felt anxious being in a totally unfamiliar house. Perhaps he was having a rough day and needed space. If I had slowed down and just watched him a little bit, then I probably would have gathered that he didn't feel comfortable around me yet. I rushed in too quickly and as a result, my "care" turned into a threat. Although I had good intentions, I caused more harm than good because I didn't take the time to observe what was really going on.

Later, I learned from the nuns that observing your subject is very important if you want to successfully help them. Paying attention to the details helps you gain wisdom for the situation at hand and to make better decisions. Whenever you desire to help your husband, you may first want to spend some time observing his ways. What approach does he respond to best? What methods turn him away? When is he in a good mood? How is he likely to react if you cut in from this particular angle? To help him, you really need to get to know him and observe him well so that you have more data to work with. If you just jump in without doing your homework and do things your own way, you could end up in a worse situation.

My husband is actually very good at observing things. No matter where we are, he'll always scan his surroundings and know everything that is going on. He'll be aware of conversations that are taking place and events that are unfolding in every corner. His keen observation skills allow him to be a very thoughtful and effective person who truly knows what others need. Like him, I want to encourage you to practice observing everything as much as you can. Be slower to rush in to things. Be still and watch first. Slowing down and being smart will get you much farther ahead in the long run. Take it from my nose.

51

Pleasing Others

After I got married, there was a relative who never seemed quite happy with me. Through his comments, I sensed that the house was never clean enough for his taste. I also got the impression that he regarded me as a lazy lump of a person. It could've all been my own faulty assumptions, but it didn't matter. I wanted to prove so badly to this person that I was a good wife and that I contributed a lot to the household. One day, after he had just come to visit and had once again made some remarks about certain things not being tidy, I decided that I was going to spend the next entire week cleaning absolutely everything I could. I was going to clean the house from top to bottom and impress the socks off this guy. It would be perfect to the point where he would have *nothing* left to say.

For the week that followed, I carried out my mission diligently and cleaned every visible surface. I put in all my efforts and really turned that house inside out. When I was done, I eagerly anticipated his next visit so that I could reap my bountiful reward of compliments. When he finally came the following weekend, I heard him enter through the garage and put his slippers on inside the house, as was his routine. I smiled to myself, giddy with excitement and even allowed him five minutes to look around. My eyes were sparkling with eagerness as I stood there alone upstairs; I could hardly wait to receive his first words.

When I eventually bounded down the stairs, he was just coming in from the garden and he looked over at me casually. "Hey Shani," he started. My eyes sparkled some more. "You forgot to wash the dog food bowl outside." Then silence. He continued walking through the house and then went upstairs to rest.

"*What?*" I said to myself. "That's all he had to say about everything I did?" My heart sank through the ground. All my efforts had gone unnoticed and like all the previous weeks before, I had once again managed to overlook something. I couldn't believe this was the outcome of everything I did. It was disappointing to say the least.

I realized at that moment, that perhaps, I could never succeed in pleasing him no matter how hard I tried. When I thought about it, I wanted to get upset. "Why is he always so negative?" "Why is he always against me?" But when I thought about it some more, I realized that *I* was the silly one. I was craving his approval and almost begging for it. I was allowing him to determine my self-worth and value. When he didn't receive me well, I felt bad about myself. I was completely putting my happiness into his hands. Why was I giving away something so valuable? And why was I trying to prove my worth to another person? The truth became strikingly clear. The problem was not my relative, or all those in the world just like him. The problem was *myself*. I needed to work on looking inwards and accepting myself first before I could convince anyone else.

My guru always taught that happiness does not come from external circumstances, it comes from within. But it was hard to understand until something actually happened to me. From that instance, I learned that when we can be happy regardless of others' opinions, then we will really have freedom to be happy no matter what.

52

The Moment

Have you ever seen toddlers at play? They can occupy themselves endlessly with nothing at all. I've seen babies completely content from just flapping their arms around, blowing raspberries or clapping their hands. I watched a baby play with a tiny piece of lint as if it were the most awesome thing in the world. They are amused by everything and stay completely submerged in the current moment. Watching them, I'm often amazed at how *present* they are. When you're with a baby, their mind is not somewhere else, thinking about tomorrow or what's going to come around next month. They're there with you, absorbed in the moment. Surprisingly, their natural behavior is aligned with the nuns' practice of being mindful wherever they are. The nuns constantly strive to be fully-engaged in the moment.

I have to admit that sadly, I am rarely present where I am. When I'm waiting at a restaurant for my food, I'll often whip out my phone and look at things that take me far away from where I am. Or if my husband is lying in bed next to me at night, I'll often choose my phone over spending time with him. It's even worse when I'm busy and start getting anxiety. My mind will race ahead, constantly thinking of what I have to do next or making lists in my head. I don't enjoy whatever I'm doing at the time since I'm so preoccupied and anxious. My presence becomes lost in the mountain of work that awaits me.

One day, while I was feeding my baby and mentally running off again, I realized that I just needed to stop and breathe. I looked down at my baby and somehow, her tiny socks caught my attention. I just stared at them, thinking how adorable they were. Then, I realized that while my thoughts were busy running off, my baby was there in my arms, occupying her tiny form and waiting for my attention if I was willing. What was I doing spending my precious time worrying about random things when I could've been focused on her? I realized that she was only going to be a baby for so long. They grow up so fast. It would be a great tragedy to miss out on her whole life simply because I couldn't *be* where I was.

Every so often, I have to lasso myself back to Earth and remember that there is nothing more important than the present moment. When that moment is gone, it is gone forever. What is life made up of, if not all those precious moments strung together? We must learn to be where we are. Otherwise, we will miss out on our lives.

53

Improvements

I tend to be very critical of myself and feel terrible whenever I do something wrong. This was made even more apparent to me one night when my family was in Las Vegas. I was eight months pregnant and taking my one-year-old around the city while my husband worked at a convention.

I wasn't used to driving around such hectic city streets, but for the sake of my daughter, I stepped outside of my comfort zone and did my best to show her around. On one of the evenings, I took her to a very popular Halloween destination. Unfortunately, we got stuck in horrid traffic on the way back. I became filled with anxiety due to all the aggressive drivers around us. Not only that, but as James waited for me at the hotel, my baby started crying and I missed my exit which landed me in even more traffic. By the time I finally made it back to our hotel, I had forgotten to bring the water jug that we all needed and had left my car in valet without giving my keys to the attendant. The valet guy had to chase me down all the way to the elevator. That was the last straw. I felt so horrible for causing someone such trouble on top of everything else. I started hating myself. My inner dialogue became so cruel and self-loathing that I was pressed hard beneath it.

A bystander who had watched the fiasco unfold by the elevator looked at me with kindness and said, "Hey, it happens." Then he added, "Your baby is so cute." It must've been the way he said it because I was suddenly flooded with his compassion and felt that, *"If strangers could be so kind to me, then why am I so hard on myself?"*

It was also at this time that I remembered what my guru had taught so often in the past. **Every day, we must spend some time to recap all the things we did well. We must note our improvements and praise ourselves so that we can progress faster.** With this thought in mind, I knew I had to go about things differently.

Putting forth an effort, I searched my brain and pursued a new route. "If I look at things in another light," I started, "I should be very proud of myself because I stepped out of my comfort zone today for the sake of my toddler. For her happiness, I put myself in a stressful scenario and got more practice doing something I never do. I became better and braver. In the end, we arrived where we needed to. We didn't get in an accident and we all got back safely. I should be proud of myself and I should also be *much* kinder to myself." I knew I really needed to put my guru's teaching to practice more.

After we got home from our trip, I tried to continue this exercise and to stop the constant harshness I felt for myself. It was important to seek out the things I did well. At first, it was difficult to see any of my daily improvements because I was so used to seeing my faults. For example, one night after an argument with my husband, I said to myself, "Shoot!

I lost my temper and left the house again." It seemed I had failed once again. It was hard to see where I had improved.

But the next day, it occurred to me that even though I still lost my temper and left the house, I came home at 12:30am instead of staying out all night like I had done once before. I spent less time being upset and didn't want to worry my husband so I brought myself back home. That was an improvement. I eagerly took note of that in my journal and praised myself for getting over my anger faster.

And that's how I began to dissect many other instances as well. Although I was often not able to act perfectly, there was usually something I could still praise myself for. It just took a little more leniency and understanding on my part.

With time, this habit became easier and at the same time I felt better about myself overall. I felt that I was improving every single day, and that gave me much encouragement to move forward. Reflecting on my improvements was like stopping at rest areas to look back and to admire all the progress I had made. The view was always beautiful. I finally understood why my teacher had prompted us to recap our improvements every day. It is necessary for the long and arduous journey to self-perfection. It accelerates growth while teaching us to be loving to ourselves.

54

Be a Good Influence

One afternoon, my husband messaged me and said, "I did something weird today." I stared at my computer and felt strange about his words. He rarely talked in such a way. Then, I could see that he was typing a response, but also that he was deleting it repeatedly as if he needed to say the words just right. I got nervous and started wondering what he could've possibly done. I braced myself for the worst.

"I helped pay for a stranger's air conditioning," he finally said.

"What?" I wrote back with a sigh of relief. "That's not something weird, that's something *kind*," I replied. He went on to explain how he came across some people who were caught in a financial bind and needed their AC unit fixed. That's when he forked up some cash out of his own pocket to help them out. I was so proud of him but he was obviously embarrassed by his behavior. Expressing kindness to strangers was new to him and he needed support from someone who could help make sense of his actions.

It occurred to me then that all my blabbering on about good deeds in the past were actually affecting him in a positive way. He was a changing form and slowly molding into all the nice people I had spoken about.

That is what this lesson is about: be a good influence on the one you love. Our influence on each other is great whether we want to admit it or not. Let us use it for something good. Encourage him to be kind to others and to make people happy. Nudge him towards his better self while helping him get in touch with his roots of virtue. He will feel an intriguing sensation at first, that feeling one gets when they know they've done something completely *good*. Then that positive feeling will spur him on to do more nice things for others. He will discover the quiet wellspring of joy that comes from helping people. In the end, he will appreciate you for adding meaning to his life and for helping him fulfill his higher purpose. He will love you more for it without even knowing why. In turn, you will admire the man he's become. Grow better hand in hand. It'll add layers of otherworldly contentment to your relationship.

55

Being Open

I know some people who are very disciplined and do a lot of good things in their lives. For example, one lady I know recycles every little thing she comes across. Another person never wastes a bite of food, even if the food is molding. They hold themselves to extremely strict standards and only expect the best from themselves. I find their self-discipline highly admirable and worthy of praise. Unfortunately, these same people I know also impose their beliefs on *others*, and as a result, drive people away from them. Instead of drawing people to them with their religious practice, they actually deter them. The truth is, no one likes to be around bossy, self-righteous people. It makes for a very unpleasant experience, even if the demands are supposedly "good." No one should ever be forced to do anything against their own will.

I used to think that the more spiritual and holy someone was, the more serious and strict they would be, just like the people I mentioned above. But actually, the longer I've been in religious institutions and observed those who are highly practiced, the more I've come to realize the opposite. Being easy-going and open is actually much harder to achieve. It's more difficult to become flexible and to constantly go with the flow of things. It takes a broad-minded perspective to accept any situation that comes to us and to let go of our own stubborn opinions.

Therefore, the more mature and learned someone is, the more inviting, friendly and open they should actually become. Crowds flock to such people because they are filled with light, warmth, and love. Being around them is a joy and comfort because they are filled with compassion and understanding.

The heart should only grow more open, not closed. The goal is to become more accommodating towards others and to become more fluid and adaptable. Thus, if you are laid back and easy-going, know that you have achieved more than you realize.

56

Unconditional Love

like taking care of people when they don't feel well. When my husband had a minor surgery on his hip and had trouble doing basic tasks, I jumped in enthusiastically with my nurse's hat. Sometimes, I had to get down on the floor to help him put on some socks and I felt happy that I could do something for him. He's always doing so much for me and my family. It was a rare and wonderful opportunity for me to serve *him*.

That's why when an old friend of mine asked if I would still be with my husband if he became handicapped or paralyzed, the answer was obvious to me. "Of course," I replied. She said that she wouldn't, with her then boyfriend, and that they had even had that actual conversation with each other. They both would leave each other.

I was surprised. The idea seemed strange to me and honestly, not very nice. She said it like it was so normal. But did it not bother her deep down that he would leave her if she wasn't well? How could it not?

It just seemed like a sad thought to me. Although in a certain way, one could think that they were making a rational decision for their lives, in my heart I felt that they had missed out on a very important point regarding love and partnership. Love should not be based upon conditions or benefits solely for one's self. The nuns taught me that love should be strong like a steel beam, unchanging and cemented firmly in the ground, able to withstand any type of calamity.

I think the question my friend asked me is a valid reflection point for anyone in a relationship and can allow one to really search their hearts for what it means to love wholeheartedly. I appreciate her question because it made me think about what kind of relationship I want to spend my life being in and it made my intentions of being with my husband so clear.

57

Seeing Beyond Our Own Pain

In the midst of conflict, it's often hard to see beyond our own pain. When we're hurting, the emotions we feel are so glaringly close that it seems to block out all other things. We think our pain makes us special, it's what we can relate to the most. But if we take a moment to listen and to understand others, we'll see that they're also struggling. They also have their own issues that they need to deal with. They may not be adept in expressing themselves, but it doesn't mean the pain isn't there.

For example, one time I got really upset at James because he was acting cranky about a party we were going to. He had agreed to go with me six months before but was now dragging his feet to go. Even when we arrived, he was tense and unable to enjoy anything. I didn't appreciate the fact that he was ruining the whole experience for me. All my anticipation from the last half year was wasted in complete disappointment. We left shortly after and I was so angry at him. We started arguing with each exchange getting louder and louder.

But all of a sudden, what happened next shocked me. Tears started streaming down my husband's face one by one. He couldn't contain his emotions anymore. I had rarely ever seen him cry. He had always made himself look so tough, but there he was unraveling before me. It was then that I fell silent. He told me that he has no time to do anything for himself. He's so stressed out and busy on the weekdays that our little bit of free time together on the weekends is so precious to him. He just wants to relax with his family at home. He explained that he hates parties and they make him feel anxious. Couldn't I be happy that he went with me already?

For the first time, I realized that he was also in pain. I was not the only one who was experiencing frustration. He was going through so much but all I could see was my own hurt. All I could relate to was myself. I didn't know anything about his circumstance. Seeing him break down broke my heart. It finally allowed me to open my eyes and to see a wounded person in front of me. All that time, I had wanted him to take away my hurt and to make me feel better. But what had I done for him? Nothing. I had not even tried to understand him. He taught me a very valuable lesson that day. I am not always the victim. Other people have feelings too and are dealing with their own struggles. I need to look beyond my own pain sometimes and realize that there may be more to the situation than what I see.

58

Faithful

When I'm out, I try not to let my eyes wander when it comes to looking at other men. I try to keep my eyes down and not look at them if they're passing me by. Perhaps that was a habit I picked up during those years when I wanted to become a nun. It is generally understood that men and women are separated in the temple and avoid all contact with each other.

Even though I didn't end up living in the temple and eventually got married, I still wanted to keep this habit as a gesture of faithfulness to my husband. I believe being faithful does not mean just physically staying by your husband's side and not running off with another man. To me, being faithful is a state of mind—not lusting after another person, not having impure thoughts, and reserving your love and affection only for the man you chose to spend your life with.

From what I've observed in myself and in others, it's too easy to cross the line between friendliness and flirting when the other gender is involved. I've seen a lot of inappropriate behavior take place under the false title of "friends." If my husband witnessed that in me, no doubt he'd be very disappointed. On the same token, if I saw him acting inappropriately with another woman, I'd be heartbroken as well. I would not be comfortable with it at all. Therefore, I try to reduce the interaction I have with men to only the ones that are necessary and I try to remain true to my husband even with all my thoughts. I think that's what he would really appreciate and desire in a wife. To me, that is the true spirit of being faithful.

59

The Bed

Try not to go to sleep unhappy. I say "try" because sometimes, it is just so difficult especially if an argument broke out right before bed. It's normal to need some time to bounce back from an argument. But if possible, try your hardest not to go to sleep unhappy because let's face it, you're not going to sleep very well anyway. With something on your mind, you'll most likely toss and turn all night, then start the next day exhausted.

If you can, try to communicate with your partner about the issue, even if the only thing you can say is what's bothering you. Try to work through it and find a solution before retreating to bed because losing a whole night of sleep is very damaging to your body and sets you up for a bad day the next day. It's best to leave unhappiness in the same day from which it came, even if you have to stay up late into the night, trying to resolve it.

Also, if you can, try not to leave the house when you're angry. Driving with enraged emotions can lead to reckless driving and impaired decision-making. Something bad could happen while you're out, and if it does, then it would be a terrible way to leave things hanging. There's too much at stake. You can take a walk in your garden or go to another room if you're upset. But try not to drive away in a furious rage while endangering your own and other people's lives. It is just not worth it. You will also save your spouse the uneasy feeling of not knowing where you are. The benefits are too numerous. Resist the temptation to leave and work strongly at staying put. Encourage your spouse to do the same. You both will not regret it.

60

Teammate

One day, my friend and I were casually walking around a bookstore and enjoying each other's company. Out of nowhere, she told me that she feels like James always "has my back" and that no matter what, he would always be on my side. She went on to tell me how her sister's husband doesn't always side with her sister, but instead with his mother or whoever he thinks is right. With James though, she had confidence that his loyalty would always be with me. What she said surprised me. I had never thought in those terms before. But I really liked what she said and felt that it was pretty nice to have my husband on my team. Upon further reflection, I also realized that, sadly, I have not always acted in the same way in return. I remember one particular incident that took place.

James' family was over at our house and as we were talking in the living room, a topic of heated debate came up. In a fit of passion, I sided with James' mom right away and scolded my husband in front of everyone. I was surprised at how strongly I felt the need to voice my opinion. However, the second I spoke, I regretted it right away. Not only had I not shown support to my husband, but I had embarrassed him in front of his family and left him on the spot. I didn't feel right about it at all even though my heart still resonated with his mom's views.

Even though James didn't say so, I felt I had betrayed him and felt deeply sorry. I had completely ditched my husband because of our differing opinions. But what probably would've been better was if I stayed quiet and discussed the matter with him later at a more appropriate time. In the company of his family, I should have stuck by him even if that meant not saying anything at all. A mother may not agree with the ways of her child, but she does not throw them to the wolves. She sticks by them and patiently sees them through any circumstance.

That day, I felt I had acted out of line. I was overtaken by anger and I had deliberately gone against my husband, hoping to show him how wrong he was. But as a mindful practitioner, that was not a nice thing to do. James would never do that to me. I learned my lesson through the uneasy feeling I got in my own stomach. I always want to be on my husband's team and to show him that my heart is with him first and foremost. We are teammates above all other things.

61

After Work

One of the biggest factors that motivated me to become a nun was the idea of impermanence. I noticed how quickly time seemed to pass and it only felt natural for me to devote my short life to self-perfection. When I become a wife, the urgency of impermanence still stuck with me. After work, I always felt that there was not much time left to spend with our loved ones. There was always the task of preparing dinner, then eating it, and cleaning it up afterward. By then, it was almost time to go to bed already. I strongly felt that it would be a waste if the precious time we had left was wasted in arguing or being unhappy with one another. We only have so much time to convey our love to our loved ones that not a moment should be wasted.

It would benefit everyone to try to make the home a happy, relaxing and cheerful place. There are enough stresses out in the world that they should not be brought home. The home should only be a retreat of healing and peace so that each person can go out the next day, ready to tackle the things expected of them.

I have witnessed too many women come home and immediately start spewing all the things that are wrong with the house. Or they'll fire off complaint after complaint about what happened during the day. That does not make for a very pleasant atmosphere. Instead, it causes more stress and unhappiness for everyone.

It would be better to come home and first greet your loved ones affectionately. Be genuinely excited to see them. Smile and put all your efforts into making them feel as loved as possible. You only have a small amount of time with them before the day is over and the opportunity is gone forever. Tomorrow always comes too soon. Therefore, try your best to make the most of the short time you're allotted after work.

62

The Video

During my religious training, I once heard a true story of a man who was always talking to his wife in a bad tone of voice. One day, as the man was in the midst of yelling at his wife again, their daughter decided to record it all on camera. No one knew about it except the little girl. After some time had passed and the incident was long forgotten, the daughter played the video back to her father one day. The father was shocked. "What? Is that me?" he asked incredulously. "I didn't know I talked like that!"

He felt rather embarrassed about his own behavior. From that time on, the father always watched himself and made sure he was not too mean when speaking to his wife.

Just like that story demonstrates, I find that we often don't know how we appear to others. When we are agitated or annoyed, we may think we have all our emotions under control. But actually, our feelings may be seeping through our actions and others can pick up on it. There have been plenty of times when my husband accused me of having a bad attitude or of having a sour look on my face. And each time, I would always deny everything, telling him that he was wrong. "You're so sensitive!" I would add. But is it possible that all those times, I just didn't know how I appeared to him and that what he was saying was true? It's very possible. Oftentimes, we just don't know what others see. After I heard the story of the man yelling at his wife, I always tried to listen to others when they feel that I am acting a certain way. Even though I may not know I'm hurting them, I try to listen to their feelings instead of shrugging them off like I used to. Their senses may be telling them something that I'm completely unaware of.

63

The Unspoken Word

A monk once told me that some horses don't need to be whipped, themselves, to learn that they need to run; they can learn the same lesson by simply watching another horse. Essentially, the monk was saying that we don't have to experience everything ourselves to learn all the lessons we need to in our lives. We can also learn from situations that occur around us. One of the lessons I've learned in such a way is the importance of holding one's tongue. Choosing to remain silent can sometimes be the most powerful message you send to somebody. It can convey so many things that words cannot.

One day, James' mom came over to our house with a bunch of food and headed right for the fridge. Our house had just undergone remodeling however and we had completely cleared out the fridge. "Why did you bring stuff over?" James said to his mom angrily. She held her tongue though and didn't say a word. She simply started putting all the food into the refrigerator.

Later, James went back to the fridge and saw that among all the food his mom had brought, there was breakfast for him which he actually needed for the next day. With our kitchen being virtually unusable, he was relieved that he had something to bring to work without our having to prepare it. In that instance, he was grateful towards his mom and I saw the guilt overcome his face.

"I'm a horrible person," he told me. He felt so bad for the way he had talked to his mom after she had done him a kind deed. Perhaps her silence on the matter contributed even more to the guilt he felt because she had not even tried to defend herself. Her tact on the matter led my husband to reflect upon his own behavior and to realize that he should've been nicer.

Another time, I was volunteering at a health-food restaurant and witnessed a similar situation. Someone had spilled some soup on the floor in the kitchen. The lady in charge saw it and turned to face the cook who was standing by it. She scolded him for leaving the spill which could have led someone to fall. Without saying a word, he quickly grabbed a towel and cleaned up the mess. Later, the lady learned that it wasn't the cook who had left the spill—it was her own daughter! Red-faced, she went to apologize to him right away and later told everyone what an admirable practitioner he was.

Watching these instances unfold before me taught me a great lesson. Holding your tongue in an upsetting situation can be extremely impactful at times. It may seem like he who remains silent during an argument is weak, but he is actually incredibly strong. Anyone can yell and babble on like a fool. It doesn't take any effort. But who can show restraint against all temptations and not utter a single word? Only the skilled and the self-disciplined.

64

Everything We Need

For several years after college, I worked as a site leader for an afterschool program. I loved the schedule because I didn't have to go to work until two o'clock in the afternoon. That meant I could stay up late every night and sleep in the next morning. Unlike me, my family had to leave early for work every morning. That always left me alone in the house for the first half of the day. One morning, while I was still sleeping, the doorbell rang. It rang several times, but I wasn't ready to get up yet so I just let it ring. I assumed it was another door-to-door salesman as they often frequented our neighborhood. Annoyed to be disturbed, I rolled over in bed, trying to go back to sleep.

Suddenly, I heard some people tampering with the back door of the house and a sickening feeling formed in my stomach. I knew instinctively that people were trying to break in. Terrified, and suddenly completely awake, I leapt out of bed and ran into the only hiding spot I knew—my parents' closet. Their closet has a pocket of space on the left side that fits one person snuggly. Entering the open closet, I crouched down in the corner, trying to make myself as small as possible. Before

I had a chance to close the door behind me, I heard footsteps running up the stairs already. They were so fast. Two men came directly into the room where I was hiding, while two more combed through other parts of the house. They were knocking down all the furniture and making so much noise which really scared me. I calculated four grown men in the house and one little ole' me. I didn't stand a chance if they found me. What were they going to do to me? I imagined all the gruesome ways in which they would torture me. I braced myself for slow and horrific pain to come. Breathless, I muttered prayer after prayer. I felt strongly that my life would end very soon and I was dizzy with fear.

Suddenly, a man came to the opening of the closet, right next to where I was hiding. He was so close; I could smell him. I felt so sick, I was going to be found out. One by one, he started taking things out of the closet. First, a box of my mom's leggings. Next, a box of sewing supplies. I was just inches away from where he was. How long was it before he reached me? The man continued removing items at a very brisk pace. And then it happened. He grabbed my ankle.

"Oh my God," I thought. "It's happening. I'm going to die."

He pulled on my ankle, thinking it was just another object. I resisted, stiff with fear. He reached for it again, and I didn't budge. Perhaps that's when he realized what it was he felt. There was a pause and then suddenly, he yelled—

"There's someone in there!" His voice shook with fear, as though he had just seen a ghost. To my surprise, I had scared him too. I heard both men drop their things (or our things, rather) and race down the stairs, running for their lives while gathering the others. Just as fast as they came, they were gone.

When it was safe, I stepped out of the closet and couldn't believe things had turned out the way they did. I was overcome with relief and gratitude. Those people were really gone and I was going to live after all.

When you have a brush against death like that, you realize how many things are normally taken for granted. In the closet just moments earlier, I would've given anything to go back to my regular life with all the mundane things in it and with all the people that I cared about. I would've even *gladly* taken back all of my problems and annoyances in life to just be alive and safe again. I realized that all the things I considered to be problems weren't actually problems. They were all trivial in the face of life and death. Whenever I was unhappy over a thing before, I had lost sight of the basic blessings granted to me. How wonderful it is to actually be breathing and well, to simply not have your life in danger.

That day, I realized that what my guru taught me is true: we already have everything we need to be happy. If we can just constantly count our blessings and remember how wonderful it is to have the gift of life, then we wouldn't get bogged down by problems so easily. We would spend less time fighting with our loved ones and more time appreciating the fact that they are even alive. This world is so unpredictable that anything can happen at any time. Being able to wake up every morning and to begin a new day is such a precious opportunity. We should be excited each time we are able to do so. Learn to always zoom out of the tiny situations that come in front of us and to see the bigger picture at hand. There is so much to be thankful for in every moment that we should always have a reason to be happy. We already have everything we need for a good life.

65

Sacrifice

The meaning of the word sacrifice involves giving up something of importance for something else regarded as *more* important. A good marriage often requires many sacrifices, but they are hard to do. As my guru stated, we're so accustomed to putting ourselves in the center of our own worlds. It's always "Me, me, me, me, me. Everything revolves around me and what I want." But when have we ever let someone else take that position? Have we ever let someone else become the object of our affections? Truly?

There is a show on television called *Naked and Afraid* where two people (a man and a woman) have to survive in the wilderness on their own for 21 days. They are not given supplies, equipment, food or even water. The only thing they can bring is a tool of their choice such as a cooking pot or a knife. Aside from that, they have to find a means to survive solely on the things they can find in nature and on the skills they have. Usually, the couple featured on the show ends up arguing and disliking each other bitterly because of the harsh situation they are thrust into. The rough terrain and dreadful conditions quickly dissolve the friendly façade that both started the show with. The end result is usually negative and ugly. They often make comments like, "I never want to see you again" or "I hate you."

One particular time however, I saw an episode that deeply inspired me. The leading pair acted in a much different manner than all the others I had seen. The woman on the team happened to be vegetarian. This was the first time I had ever seen a vegetarian attempt this type of challenge and I was intrigued because hunting is quite heavily emphasized on the program. Throughout the episode, you could see the woman picking berries and examining the plants in her surroundings. Her male partner would go out to hunt and share his catch with her each time. But she would always politely decline, sometimes with an uneasy look on her face which she couldn't help. The sight of the animals, even if they were tiny, seemed to trigger her disgust. At one point, the guy killed a long snake and again offered her some. She said she wouldn't eat it. But if he needed, she could help him prepare it.

When she said that she could help him prepare the snake, I was filled with surprise and awe. For someone who looked so grossed out from just the thought of eating little insects, it was incredible that she could 1) put her own feelings aside and 2) offer to help her partner prepare a huge snake for his meal. Gutting an animal is hard enough for someone who eats meat, let alone a vegetarian who most likely loves animals. I was a vegetarian for most of my life and don't think I would have had the courage to offer what she did. For her partner's sake, she was willing to overcome her own feelings of discomfort in order to make his life easier. The scene inspired me greatly as I finally saw two people working selflessly together to finish the challenge. Their tolerance and consideration towards each other was so rare.

Oftentimes, we refuse to help others when our interests collide. We cap our own rules onto other people and expect them to act according to how *we* feel. But to put aside what we're comfortable with in order to make another person's life more comfortable? That is true kindness. It would be nice if we could follow in that woman's footsteps and practice placing others in a position of importance. I've found that the best love stories are always built on sacrifice and loving dedication towards one another.

66

The Cushion

My husband and I were driving on the freeway one Mother's Day when all of a sudden, a police car started weaving through the lanes to slow traffic. "Seriously? Right now?" my husband asked impatiently. It seemed like we were being made late to our destination for no apparent reason. Eventually, traffic stopped completely as the police car parked itself in one of the lanes. We grew ever the more impatient as we just waited there. Then, the police man exited his vehicle and ran out onto the open freeway. He started lugging a giant cushion off the road which was only now visible to us. He was actually removing a hazardous object off the freeway so that we could proceed safely. When we realized what he was doing, we felt bad for thinking negatively about him. He was actually doing us a service and trying to keep us safe.

A lot of times, we don't know the intentions of others and just naturally assume the negative. If someone acts in a way that we don't understand, we often think the worst. For example, if someone doesn't respond to a message we send out in a prompt manner, we may be inclined to think that they don't like us. They're avoiding us. The nuns refer to this type of thinking as "Fei li zuo yi," in Chinese. But the truth of the matter is, we don't know. We don't know what other people are thinking or what situation they are caught up in. We have no frame of reference. So why should we assume the worst? Why make ourselves feel bad when there could be a million possible explanations? We should give others the benefit of the doubt and think in a more positive manner.

One night, I was bothered that my husband didn't invite me to his company dinner. It seemed like all the wives of the other employees were going. I felt myself get negative and assume the worst. "He's embarrassed of me," I started to think. But before I could spiral further into negativity, I decided to ask my husband directly. "Why didn't you invite me to your company dinner?" I asked him. "Because I invited you before and you didn't want to go," he replied. I had forgotten all about that instance. Had it really happened? Probably. I felt rather embarrassed. The cause had been myself and *not* because my husband was ashamed of me. I had put myself through unnecessary pain for no reason; there had been a perfectly good explanation. So next time you find yourself not knowing the reason for a situation, try not to assume the worst, though it may be tempting. Just for fun, try to assume the positive. You might just be right.

67

The Break

One thing I learned from the nuns is that if something provokes you to the point where you are burning up with anger, it is best to leave the scene first to recollect yourself.

For example, when my husband and I fight and someone starts cussing, then I know things are going to get really bad really fast. I've observed through my own past arguments with him that cussing is the first sign of the argument escalating to dangerous levels; between the two of us, someone is about to lose control. Now when that sign appears, I know it is my cue to take a break from the scene before some serious damage takes place. Sometimes, I'll excuse myself politely, but other times, I'll just leave without saying a word. It's the best I can do at the moment.

When things are so intense like that, I've found that taking a break from the source is very beneficial because it can prevent really bad things from happening. Obviously two people are caught up in the heat of the moment and good judgement is severely impaired. It's hard to have a good result out of pure, crazy emotions like that. Wisdom is hindered when we're so angry.

Thus, I've learned that leaving the scene and taking a break can help calm me down and allow me to think more rationally. I can start contemplating ways to handle the rest of the situation better. When emotions aren't stirred up so much, I can finally access the wisdom that's hidden deep inside. As my teacher once said, "When the water is clear, we can see the fish inside."

68

Connections

One year, shortly after the new year had begun, I found out that a distant relative of mine had been paying for a huge chunk of my living expenses. Prior to that, I had always thought someone else in my family was taking care of it. I felt so bad because I had never cared much for this relative who I now found out had been paying for my comfort and luxury throughout the years. In fact, to be honest, I didn't even much *like* this person but he was contributing largely to the well-being of my life. How oblivious and truly ungrateful I had been for so long.

Much like that instance, I often find that we are unaware of others' contributions to our lives. The nuns told me that we should constantly hold gratitude in our hearts for others and reflect upon how we are all connected. But how often do we actually do this? How often do we think of the people who grow our food or even those who manufacture our pencils? It's hard to see the efforts of those outside our normal spheres, or to hold gratitude for those who supply everyday things for us. For example, we tend to think that as long as we can purchase something, it's our given right to possess it. But actually, it took someone's hard work to make that object exist. Someone had to first come up with the idea behind it, and then find a way to physically produce it. Sometimes, large factories and large networks of people are involved in the production of just a single item. But oftentimes, this fact is overlooked and we think we are completely self-sufficient.

There is a dried cheese snack I enjoyed eating during my stay in Taiwan. It was easily purchased in every part of Taiwan that I visited, so I took it for granted, thinking that it was the *company's* privilege that I was even buying their product. However, after I returned to America, I couldn't find those same cheese snacks anywhere even though I lived close to numerous Asian markets. Now, whenever I crave them, I think about how lucky people in Taiwan are. It is actually their good fortune to be able to buy this product so easily and to have it so readily available. Nothing should ever be taken for granted.

Looking at all the goods and services around us, we are really indebted to so many people; more than we can imagine. This applies even more so to the people living immediately around us who directly affect and support us on a daily basis. We are all intricately connected and we should constantly hold a grateful heart towards everyone and everything.

69

"I Agree"

've noticed something peculiar that happens time and time again. Whenever my husband says something negative about me and I actually tell him that I agree with him, he'll soften up completely saying, "Now now…" and then start to defend me.

For example, if my husband complains about me being too soft as a parent and I agree with him, further adding, "Yeah, I'm too soft with our daughter. You're a much better parent than me," then he'll completely flip his stance and comfort *me*. "No, I'm not a better parent at all. Actually, our child needs someone like you sometimes to find comfort in. I'm too mean," he'll say. Not only will he defend me, but he'll often reflect upon himself and shed light upon his own shortcomings. I've noticed this happening too many times that I've come to expect it like clockwork. I am not sure why this happens. Perhaps, he lets down his guard when I don't get defensive and challenge him. That leaves him with no argument to protect. The more I accept his critiques without being defensive, the more he'll soften up and try to comfort me, completely abandoning his standpoint. Because I've adopted his opinion, he'll start to adopt mine. And then something beautiful happens—two people defending each other and unveiling the good that is actually present in the situation. I find that this approach is much more tactful than reverting to anger. Nuns are always trying to find more diplomatic ways of handling a tough situation and I'm glad I found this method that works. Next time your spouse hurls a negative comment at you, try agreeing with him without getting defensive and see for yourself what happens. It's quite amusing.

70

New Hobbies

"Want to go play ping pong?" my husband asked one morning.

I groaned inside my mind. "No, not really," I thought. Playing sports is not exactly my thing. I don't find it fun and I struggle a lot with hand-eye coordination. But I knew he wanted to play ping pong for a long time now. It also occurred to me that broadening my horizons would be good for me and that I should try to be a good sport.

"Alright," I replied, getting out of bed. It would be my first time playing.

Together, we went to an indoor ping pong court in the area. Luckily, nobody was there so I wouldn't have to make a fool of myself in front of other people. We unloaded our gear by a table and quickly got started. My husband served a ball to me and to my great surprise, I returned it. We went back and forth, hitting the ball to each other and it wasn't as hard as I thought.

"Hey, you're pretty good at this," he said and I actually agreed with him. I enjoyed hearing the sound of the plastic ball hitting my paddle. It was very gratifying and gave me more confidence with each hit. We played for a while and in the end, I decided that I quite enjoyed playing ping pong. It was so fun. James wanted to leave already, but I wanted to stay longer. I was just getting started.

There have been many times, where I have been reluctant to try something at first but ended up completely loving every second of it. My interests eventually expanded to many boy-ish things, thanks to my husband. I raced in go-carts and watched my pink sweater get splattered in mud from our ATV. I drove a remote-control car through a running stream and shot zombies with guns at an arcade. My mind was exposed to many new activities and as a result, I feel more well-rounded today because my areas of weakness have all been sharpened.

Although my intentions were always to make my husband happy at first, I usually wound up getting more out of it than him. Being open to things has really broadened my mind and allowed me to see much more of the world. It has also made me a better conversationalist as I can relate to more people with my new hobbies. I've since learned that I should just put down my stubborn resistance to his suggestions and embrace all the new things he plans for us. It is a pity to close a door to a new world.

My openness has also made him more willing to try the activities I suggest to him. He has come to enjoy things he probably wouldn't have enjoyed on his own, like exploring nature, watching musical plays and attending concerts. Our willingness to try for each other has brought us closer.

I'd like to encourage you to also step out of your comfort zone and to try something new. Don't be afraid. Dive in and experience a new challenge. If nothing else, do it for his happiness. Most likely, you will not be able to keep the happiness from yourself.

71

Diary

For as long as I can remember, I've kept a diary. My favorite kind as a child were the ones with locks. There, I knew my thoughts were *really* safe. I'd pour out my feelings onto the pages and recount every little detail of my childhood days. They were a constant companion, and in them, I bore my soul. The diaries I kept as a child were lost. But the ones I started in high school, all the way up to now, have remained with me and are considered some of my most cherished possessions. I have almost seventy diaries to date, all sitting in chronological order on my closet shelf. Now, the habit of writing is so ingrained in me that it seems unnatural to go days without writing.

Through the years, they have kept me sane and acted as a container for all my thoughts much like a therapist. When there were things I couldn't tell a soul, I knew I could confide in my diary at any time and empty my heart out unto it. This simple habit made me a more disciplined person as I was able to sort out my thoughts better after releasing them all on a blank sheet of paper. By writing out the matters of my heart into a giant brainstorm, I could then begin to organize my thoughts and to see where the real problems were. It just made everything so clear.

Even as I read back on past diaries, I could always see what my recurring issues were and where I needed to make improvements. They have been an extremely helpful guide to make myself better and to see myself in a clearer light. There are many things we can't see when we are stuck up close in a situation, as we get so caught up with all the feelings and emotions in front of us. But when we read about the same situation from a third-person point of view, it makes everything easier to understand because we are further removed from the situation. We can always see things easier when we are outside of it. That is why it helps to write things down. Later, I was delighted to find that my late teacher also kept diaries which he later passed down to our current guru. I imagine the act of writing had similar benefits for him as well and helped him become a more contemplative person.

Often, through the process of writing, I have also received thoughts of inspiration which have moved me and helped me to think more positively. It's like a portal into a wiser version of myself which constantly prods me to think in a more mature way. I strongly encourage you to start a diary of your own for all the reasons I have mentioned. It is one of the fastest and surest ways to self-improvement. Your husband and you will both benefit from the simple habit and it barely takes any effort.

72

The Boss

I've been with James for a third of my entire life. Needless to say, he is very close to my heart. He can bring out the very best in me and at the same time, he can access deep reserves of anger I didn't even know I had. When we fought in the past, I noticed I would easily spiral out of control because he was someone I cared about so deeply and his actions would affect me just as much. I didn't like losing my temper but it seemed so hard to manage at times.

That is, until one day, I heard an audio CD recorded by the wife of my sister's pastor. In it, she was giving parenting advice. She mentioned that some parents would lose their patience with their children and resort to unnecessary aggression. She said it's easy to get mad and frustrated, but it *is* also possible for us to keep our composure. Just look at those in the work force. No matter how upset one gets at their boss, they know to show restraint because they are in a professional environment. Not only that, but if they lose control, they could lose their job. The consequences are too great. So in fact, people are capable of exercising control, even under upsetting circumstances.

After I heard that, I never forgot her message again. I was filled with hope because what she said rang true to me. I agreed that we *are* capable of containing our emotions because we have demonstrated that time and time again in the workplace. I vowed that the next time I got mad at my husband, I would pretend that we were in a professional, working environment. How would I react to him then?

Although the advice I heard was meant for parenting, it has actually helped tremendously in my marriage since that time. It constantly reminds and encourages me of the restraint I'm capable of.

73

Equilibrium

Nature's ways are often fascinating to me. Did you know that we are attracted to the smell of someone who has vastly different immunity genes than our own? That might explain why we are not attracted to the smell of say, our own dads. Because their genetic makeup is too similar to ours. We are drawn to those who are different which is nature's way of ensuring healthy offspring. Where we are weak, the other person is strong. And where they are weak, we are strong. By merging two people who complement each other, the healthiest offspring is formed.

It occurred to me one day that this concept doesn't just apply to our physical make up, it apples to our emotional make up as well. What do I mean? Well, my husband is direct, honest and straightforward. I am sensitive, emotional and indirect. Our personality types seem to rest on opposite sides of the spectrum. But when we got married, we had to merge our personalities together to reach a healthy balance. He had what I needed and I had what he needed. I learned to become stronger and to stand up for myself as he learned to back down and become softer in his approach. After reaching an equilibrium, we were both made better in every way and were then able to pass down improved personality traits to our children. Essentially, by merging with our opposites, we became stronger and could then give away better qualities to the next generation. The benefits were visible both in the present and in the future.

I bring up these points because after getting married, the differences often stand in the way of us getting along. We tend to see differences between one another as obstacles that need to be conquered. But from what I've learned in the temple, each person's differences are actually a thing of beauty and add to the benefit of the collective community. Dealing with different temperaments acts as magnets pulling us to the center of ourselves, making us more grounded. So instead of shunning the ways in which we differ, we should embrace them and see it all as nature's design to make us better.

74

Until You've Been There...

I was a goody two-shoes my whole life. Never drank, never did drugs, rarely partied. I liked to follow the rules and stay within the confines of safety at all times. That's why when I watched those intervention shows on TV showing people nearly dying from drug overdose or from cutting themselves, I simply couldn't understand it. It seemed unthinkable to do that to one's body. I would always ask myself, "*Why?*" "Doesn't that hurt?" It seemed so weird to me. But one night, all of that changed.

It was Saturday, a night where everyone was probably out doing something fun and exciting. But I was having a bad night. In fact, I was having a night where I felt like killing myself. My mood was dangerously low and I felt trapped inside my own body. It was about 11:30pm, almost time for bed. But I couldn't go to sleep. I had a belly full of anger and depression that I didn't know what to do with. So in

112

an attempt to escape my feelings, I went driving. I didn't know where to go, I just knew I needed to go somewhere. It was during this time that I suddenly wanted to go to a bar and drink; take the edge off. Isn't that what everyone always does in the movies when they're upset? So I really did. I drove to a place I knew and ordered myself a drink at the bar.

After several sips, I felt my body go numb and relax. I watched the TV hanging on the wall and felt my sadness dissipate. It felt good. It felt wondrously good and at that point, I finally understood why some people turn into alcoholics. It's tempting to want to take the easy way out and to drink the pain away. Experiencing my moment of weakness made me understand the weakness in others. "Ah-ha." A lightbulb went off inside my head. All these years, I had been judging others for their actions, but I couldn't understand them at all until it happened to me. I couldn't understand them until I hit a low—a low lower than low that finally triggered me to act recklessly.

I've learned that I should never judge anyone for how they act. I am in no place to judge. I don't know what others are going through, I am not God. I don't know what state of mind they're consumed in. If I were in their shoes, could I deal with things any differently? I don't know. I just don't know until it happens to me. Therefore, I should never judge a single person including my husband. Sometimes, I blame him for not being patient enough or for being short-tempered. But what if I were him? What if I grew up under his circumstances and had to deal with a rocky childhood? Would I be able to do any better? Not knowing the answer to this question reminds me to stay humble and to never judge.

75

Appreciation

Nothing seems to kill enthusiasm quite like the lack of appreciation. Back when I still had a fear of cooking and found it intimidating to even step foot in the kitchen, I had a brief moment of inspiration to conquer my fear. I wanted to cook dinner for someone as a heartfelt gesture for their kindness towards me. I went to the market and picked up an impressive array of fresh vegetables and ingredients. Hurrying home, I went to work right away—washing, chopping and dicing. Because of my lack of experience, it took me nearly the whole afternoon just to complete my dish. It was quite a triumphant moment when I tasted the finished product and decided that I liked it. I felt I had overcome a huge hurdle and accomplished something that was personally hard for me. I couldn't wait to unveil my surprise and to show off the fact that I had *cooked* something.

When my guest of honor finally came home and I presented what I had made, my heart was sorely crushed when he looked over at me in utter disappointment and said, "What? There's no meat?" Clearly, he had no interest in eating my creation at all despite the fact that I had poured so much of my love, time, and courage into it. It was a deflating moment and I felt like I never wanted to cook for him again. That's when I experienced how much a lack of appreciation can kill one's motivation and prevent it from wanting to move forward in a positive direction.

On the other hand, I have also witnessed how much a show of appreciation can propel one forward. In my teaching career, when particular students have demonstrated their appreciation for the things I taught, I felt my whole being fill up with happiness and gain incredible newfound energy. I wanted to give my all to those students because they were appreciative of my efforts and made me feel like my time was not being wasted. Although teachers should not have favorites, I couldn't help but always gravitate more towards those grateful students and want to give them more. It's only human nature. Nuns constantly practice holding a grateful heart and after that instance, I could clearly see why. Appreciation always draws more good things to it. By showing gratitude, you will surely get more of what you want and make others happy to do things for you. Put this secret into practice and you will naturally become everyone's favorite.

76

Compliments

During the first trimester of my second pregnancy, I was feeling really drained from nausea and fatigue. My husband and I were out and decided to visit a juice bar so that I could get hydrated. I went up front to pay, feeling the dryness of my lips and the weakness overtaking my body. Totally caught off guard, the service girl suddenly said to me, "You're gorgeous."

"What?" I asked, a bit confused behind my make-up free face. I had heard her but didn't quite believe my ears. "You're gorgeous," she repeated with a smile on her face. I was so flustered that my husband later told me that I started rubbing my face very awkwardly. It's not every day someone makes a comment like that. And it was extra shocking given how completely unattractive I felt. But as the day continued, I started feeling different. I felt sheepishly happy and even had an air of elevated confidence. I would look in the mirror with curiosity, wondering what she had seen. She brightened up my mood considerably.

I know that nuns are always encouraged to speak positively of others. But it wasn't until I came into contact with that girl when I understood the importance of doing so. Words are so easy to speak but their impact can be so great. I felt it first-hand when I was given a random compliment back at the store. That tiny event spurred me to think about the effects of compliments and how happy they can make people. I wanted to follow in that girl's footsteps and spread happiness to others with my words. I realized how little I compliment people and what a pity that is. My loved ones certainly deserve to be complimented more often. How many things do we leave unsaid? How many things do we feel but not express? When was the last time I told my husband he was handsome and wonderful? I couldn't remember.

Things became different after that day. A nice girl at a juice bar had given me a personal lesson on something the nuns had been preaching to me for years and I intended to take that lesson far into my life. From what I've observed since, people can generally benefit from a kind word or two. Compliments can always lift people up much higher than we expect. We should invest a genuine effort into always keeping a nice word at the tip of our tongues, ready to dispense at any given moment. It is one of the easiest acts of kindness we can employ, yet the effects are so far-reaching.

77

Differences

Although men and women are fundamentally human beings at the core, I have found some subtle differences that exist between the two genders. Or at least between my husband and I. For example, I am a very vocal person and like to talk about everything I go through. When I have a bad day, it especially helps for me to talk about what happened and to get things off my chest. It's like my way of dumping all the trash that I've been holding onto all day. Afterwards, I am always happy again and can go on with my life.

My husband, on the other hand, doesn't enjoy talking about his problems. He doesn't like to recap bad things that happen and tries his hardest to forget about them. After work, he refuses to talk about more work and just leaves everything at the office. Therefore, when he listens to my complaints from all throughout the day, he processes them differently than I would; he actually internalizes them. Instead of just letting my words go in one ear and out the other as I do, he holds on to the negativity. He gets stressed over my problems and thinks I'm asking for help to fix everything. But that is not what I want from him. I just need him to listen.

That is just one way in which he and I differ. When I found out that my actions were being a burden on him, I tried to be more mindful of my behavior. Instead of venting all of my frustrations out onto him after a long day of work, I would choose to do so at a better time or to remind him before speaking that I only need him to listen and nothing else. It always helps when I remind him first.

I've found that noting these little differences between us has helped me understand my husband better and to create more harmony in our relationship. We are all human beings, but we each have our own preferences. If we can be sensitive to others' views, then the relationship can be stronger.

78

The Never-Ending Book

My mother informed me one day that my aunt would be visiting us in America from Taiwan. I was excited because my aunt had taken care of me during my time abroad and I had always felt grateful to her. I couldn't wait to see her and show her around. When I told my husband about her coming, however, he was less than enthusiastic. In fact, he seemed downright bothered that I would spend time outside of my schedule with her. He even started telling me reasons why he didn't like her and I was puzzled because they had barely even met.

At first, I wanted to get upset because I felt that he was being unreasonable. My aunt rarely ever made the trip to the States. Why was James being difficult about it? But then later that night, it occurred to me that this was not the first time he had gotten bothered by family-related events. And actually, now that my awareness was on the subject, I saw that James had a pattern of feeling uncomfortable whenever family matters were involved. Then, it hit me like a ton of bricks. James experienced a lot of family-related traumas growing up. Somehow, the topic must hit a painful nerve in him.

I still didn't fully understand him and my speculations were still only that, speculations. But I remembered what my guru once said: *Each person is such a complex being. Each heart is so vast and intricate like a limitless universe. Reading each person is like reading a never-ending*

118

book—it would take lifetimes to understand. So instead of getting mad at my husband that day and thinking I already knew everything there was to know about him, I decided to remain curious about his life and to only try to understand him more. I tried to humble myself in order to read his story better and to unravel the layers that are buried deep within him. I find that this approach really allows my compassion to shine through and not my short temper. It shifts me into a mode of understanding rather than judgement which really softens how I view him. It only makes me want to uncover the mystery further and to read his book better.

79

Excuses

I have a bad habit of always making excuses for myself when others point out something I did wrong. My first instinct is to defend myself and think of reasons to justify what I did. I often deflect the blame automatically without even taking the time to truly reflect upon the situation and to evaluate if I really *was* at fault. That is a habit that actually goes against what the nuns work towards, though, and only shows how much I want to protect my pride. What if I was able to set my pride aside? What if I was able to own up to my mistakes without a second word?

I had a friend who was able to do this. There was a time when I was not happy with her. She had done a series of things to upset me and feeling bothered, I finally confronted her one day. She listened to everything I had to say without interrupting once and seemed to be taking it all in. At the end, when I was done, she simply said that she was sorry for all that she had done. And that was that. She didn't try to deflect the blame or make excuses for herself. She simply owned up to every mistake she made and said sorry. I found that her reaction was refreshing and made interacting with her very pleasant even amidst an uneasy situation. I was immediately rid of all anger and even felt relieved that she had been such a good listener. If she had made excuses or denied things, which was what I was expecting, I would have felt annoyed. But her responsibility to receive the blame and to apologize not only made me forgive her right away, it made me respect her more, especially when I looked back on the matter years later. Her maturity in handling an uncomfortable situation really left an impression on me.

Now, when I find myself tempted to shield myself from blame, I'll sometimes be reminded of that example and try to refrain from such behavior. It's just not pleasant. If I'm at fault, it's much better to accept it and apologize. Then everyone can go on with their lives. It's really not a big deal at all.

80

The Chest

Everything you do is a representation of yourself. People will look at what you do and form opinions about you whether you realize it or not. For example, if you dress sloppily at work, people may start to lose respect for you even though you exhibit a friendly demeanor. What they see is often more powerful than anything else and they may be inclined to make judgements. If your front yard is messy and overtaken by weeds, you are sending out a certain message to others. Or if you deliver a report to your boss that is laden with errors, you are sending out another message. Everything you do is a show of your character and that is why you should do everything to the best of your ability. Try not to slack, even in tiny, seemingly insignificant tasks. When you're folding laundry, make it a point to fold each piece of clothing beautifully. It is a representation of who you are. When you're putting away a blanket, make sure to match the corners and fold it nicely so that it looks neat. It shows who you are. Everything you do is an opportunity to show the world who you are and you should always showcase the best version of yourself. You will automatically command respect by doing so.

I remember once, a monk was speaking at an event. He told us how our late teacher had asked him to mop a room in their living quarters. The monk did so right away and mopped the room as best as he could. When the teacher returned, he moved aside a chest, as a test, to see if his disciple had gone through the trouble of cleaning underneath it. Fortunately, he did. He passed the test. The monk told us how relieved he was to have done that and how he would continue to do so every time after that.

He might not have known it at the time, but that simple action spoke volumes about his inner standards of excellence. Even when nobody was watching, he did things to the best of his ability. And when it was found out, it left a strong impression on everyone. Now, whenever I clean, I try to reach every surface like he did, even if no one is physically hovering over me to watch. I feel good just knowing that what I put out there is the best that I'm capable of.

81

The Game

In high school, we were often required to take standardized tests and I always dreaded them. They seemed like such a chore. However, in college, I trained myself to enjoy them. How? Instead of thinking of them as tests, I began thinking of them as a game; something that people actually enjoy. I pictured each question to be part of a challenge and I could use different strategies to eliminate the wrong answers. If I got a problem correct, then I could advance to the next level and gain more points. It was more exciting that way.

I find that similarly, life often gives us problems that are comparable to tests. We are given hurdles that must be overcome before we can move forward. They're not always fun, just like those standardized tests, but if we change the way we see them, then the entire experience can be different. For example, one time I was putting the dishes away and my husband made a comment that annoyed me. Instead of defaulting to annoyance and regarding it as something unpleasant, I told myself, "Okay, the opportunity is here. I've been met with a challenge. What strategy can I use to overcome it?" I viewed the situation as a bump in the road that just made the course a little more interesting. In the end, I threw on my imaginary cape and envisioned my teacher looking over the entire scene. "Watch me now," I thought. I wanted to make my teacher proud.

If there's one thing I learned at the temple, it's that: the hardships that come to us can actually be the components that teach us the most in life and help us to become wiser and more mature than we were. Problems have the ability to strengthen us and to stretch us out in ways that nothing else can. If the "game" is played right, we can actually launch much further ahead in life and come out winning. Therefore, life's tests can be viewed as a game that can yield extraordinary benefits. It throws us into the arena and begs the question, "Do you have what it takes?"

Next time you find yourself stuck in something unpleasant, try changing your mind around. Now you are faced with a problem or a challenge. How can you proceed so that you can beat the game and advance to the next level?

82

Efficiency

One thing that surprised me while staying at the temple was how everyone not only tried to get things accomplished, but also tried to do them *well* and *quickly*. It wasn't enough that a meal was cooked. It also had to be done with efficiency and quality. That was just the standard of our teacher. Coincidentally, my husband also likes the word efficiency. He even finds it sexy. Perhaps his job as a manager has something to do with it. He doesn't like to see wasted effort or time. In a large company, where so many things must get done each day, efficiency really becomes key. When things aren't running efficiently, money is wasted. Resources are wasted. Time is wasted.

I find that in a marriage, efficiency is also very applicable and useful especially where conflict is involved. During an argument, a lot of time and energy is often wasted on unnecessary drama. Emotions spin out of control, things are taken personally and childish bickering often occurs. But if two people can take *all* of their energy and simply concentrate it on finding a solution to the problem, then so much time and sanity would be spared. That time could be spent living happily and enjoying life, as life is short enough.

Some arguments are so long, drawn out and exhausting because they are not handled efficiently. It would be so much better if each person could identify the problem at hand, then channel their energy into finding a way out of that problem. The whole ordeal could be quick and painless. Then both people could move on. However, that type of behavior takes maturity and mutual respect.

Sometimes, when my husband and I are fighting, I'll suddenly recognize that I'm being immature and that I'm stirring up an unnecessary storm based on my emotions. I'll catch myself playing games or trying to "punish him" because my feelings are hurt. But I am not addressing the real issue and discussing the core problem. Neither of us are. That's when I know time is being wasted and this argument could be handled in a better way. It takes practice to become more efficient at fighting but it definitely gets easier over time. Just remember, focus on fixing the problem at hand and nothing else. Move towards a solution and stick to your goal. Fighting may be inevitable, but prolonged suffering doesn't have to be.

83

The Net

When one person improves, everyone else around them naturally improves too. If you start acting with virtue in everything you do, you'll soon start to notice a shift in others. They will begin to take on your behaviors and use them in their own lives. Their quality of living will be elevated simply because you raised the bar of excellence and demonstrated how a mature and admirable adult should act. It is like a net. When one part of a net is raised, the rest of the net will follow because of all the links that connect one to the other. In our lives, people are also connected by invisible links. When one person improves, all the "links" in that person's "net" will also improve.

Often, in my teaching career, I've seen just *one* teacher alter the entire climate of the whole school. This teacher is usually hard-working, dedicated and adored by all the students; a sort of super star on campus. Because all the other teachers don't want to fall too far behind, they'll try to improve their own teaching practices to try to match up to that one super star teacher. Call it a bit of friendly competition if you like. But whatever the case, no one likes to fall too far behind. Everyone wants to stay in the game.

Therefore, one person acting out in excellence can cause others to rise up dramatically. By simply working on yourself and purifying your actions, you are already helping all the people around you to improve their own lives. They will watch you and emulate you. When you respond calmly to rudeness and they see themselves acting out childishly, they will make a comparison and see that they're falling short. Over time, they will understand the value of your behavior, while slowly casting out their immature ways. You become a pioneer without even having to teach anyone anything. All you have to do is work on yourself. Focus on walking more towards the light, on responding with kindness rather than anger. Use virtue as your compass and soon, you will help everyone around you simply by being who you are.

84

Self-Love

As I reflect back on my life, the most difficult period I went through was middle school. Although they were just three short years and I was young, my confidence took a traumatic blow during that time. I don't believe I've ever fully bounced back from all the bullying and backstabbing that took place then. It was such an awful time of my life filled with social isolation and condemnation. The anxiety and pain carried on into my adult life and I never really felt comfortable being around a lot of people. For the longest time, I blamed my bullies for ruining my life. I blamed them for shattering my self-esteem and for leaving me with so much fear.

But one day, as I watched an interview of a famous singer, my perception on this completely changed. This singer was a *beautiful* woman who was shockingly talented and charismatic. On the show, she revealed how she got picked on as a little girl because she was half white and half black. People teased her for not fitting into one specific category. Mixed children were rarer in those days and she stood out from the others. This sweet girl grew up thinking she was worthless and flawed because others bullied her. However, all I could see staring back at me on the screen was this stunningly attractive woman. She couldn't see what a jewel she was, yet it was so obvious to me and perhaps to the rest of the world. She was so lovely but sadly, she didn't believe it so eventually, she led others to not believe it as well. If she had known what a treasure she was, she wouldn't have let anyone get inside her head and talk her down. But I'm guessing she suffered from low-confidence to begin with, so she let others' criticism in. She digested their hateful words, resulting in a life full of unhappiness and shame.

Her story made something click in my head. I was always blaming my bullies for my pain. But it was actually *me* who let them in; it was my mentality. I was already filled with guilt and didn't love myself before the bullies were ever in the picture. Upon further examination, I actually feel that I *invited* those bullies in with my energy and my demeanor. When it came down to it, *I* was always the one that didn't accept myself. Others are not to blame. I hold the key. Only I can liberate myself.

The more I live, the more I realize that *so many* things all boil down to self-love. Do you love yourself? Do you have a healthy vision of yourself? What behaviors are you willing to tolerate from others?

This is one of the most important factors to achieving happiness in your life. I really can't stress enough how self-love is the answer to so many of life's problems. *You* are the key and not anyone else. You are the only one who can free yourself. That is great news because you already have everything you need to turn your life around. You don't have to depend on an object outside of yourself. You already possess the tools you need to live the life you want.

Loving yourself is not a one-day affair though. Sometimes it takes years and years to reverse the effects of past negative thinking. One thing that's helped me a lot is keeping a journal by my bedside. Every day, I write down five *different* things I love about myself. They might include things I did well that day, my improvements, personality traits that I admire or just simply telling myself that I'll never let anyone treat me badly. Doing so has really helped elevate my self-image and allowed me to cherish myself more. Learn to be your own biggest cheerleader, lifting yourself up when no one else will. I know that the real path to happiness begins with me and that loving myself is so crucial to healthy living.

85

Femininity

In society, women are often associated with negative traits such as: narrow-mindedness, drama and jealousy. Even in many religious sects, women are often seen as being in a place of disadvantage when compared to men. But what I feel is that women possess wonderful traits that aren't stressed enough. For example, one thing I love about women is their tendency towards gentleness. Women are often sensitive, sympathetic and nurturing which, to me, are *amazing* strengths. They're beautiful qualities that bring warmth, power and healing to others.

I know that I'm a very sensitive person. The littlest things can make me cry. I used to be ashamed of this but I've come to realize that it's part of what makes me powerful as well. My sensitivity connects me to others and makes me more understanding of their situations. My sensitivity allows me to comfort others better and to heighten my compassion, which the world so desperately needs. These feminine qualities are so valuable and should be embraced.

In my home, I really try to be as sympathetic and caring towards my husband as I can. I remind myself that his mother, who used to play the nurturing role in his life is no longer living with him. She passed that role on to me when I married him. If not me, then who else can watch over her beloved son? There's no one left. I'm the only one who can fulfill this important job. I remind myself that my husband has been entrusted to *me* for my caretaking and that I can really use my strengths as a woman to make his life better.

Embrace your feminine qualities and let them shine. Allow others to gain from the sweet traits that make you uniquely you. Be proud of your womanhood and put your gifts to use. The people around you could surely benefit from a loving and gentle role model in their lives.

86

Manners

had a friend who always seemed to be yelling at his mom on the phone. One time, I was able to be in the presence of both of them and again, they were yelling at each other. After the mom left, I asked, "Is everything okay? You guys seem upset." And he replied, "Oh no, everything's fine. That's just how we talk to each other."

I was rather surprised because they were being so mean. Although he said that was just how they talked to each other, I'm pretty sure no one likes to be talked to that way. It's simply not pleasant. My guru always taught that if we can be kind and courteous to people on the street, then surely, we should be able to exercise the same manners on our loved ones. In the end, our family members are the ones who get to see whether we are truly nice people or not. We may be able to fool outsiders, but not our families.

I think the problem is that familiarity and comfort often give the illusion that we can become sloppy with those we're used to being around. "It's okay to be rude because they're family. They'll always stick by me," we might think. We start to take their presence for granted and become lazy with our basic manners.

But perhaps we should work at being politer to our loved ones. After all, they have done the most for us and deserve the most. We should save our best behaviors for them. If we can't, then every kindness we show others would be fake. Our priorities would be all askew.

I used to be just like that. Around my friends, I would act sugary sweet. I was terrified of making them unhappy in any way. But with my family, I often spoke in a bad attitude and didn't care about their feelings. My mom pointed this out to me one day and I resisted her comment at first. It made me uncomfortable. But over time, I thought about it more and realized that I was indeed being double-sided.

In the end, I realized that our families deserve to be treated with kindness and respect just like anyone else. It's important to remember to say "please" and "thank you" even though it may seem trivial and unnecessary at times. You started off being a sweet sugar plum to your husband, exercising the highest level of good manners that you were capable of, and he couldn't resist you. It would be a shame if that sugar plum turned into a rude and sour grape as I've often seen happen in other people's marriages. Politeness is always appreciated by everyone. We should try to say our words in a nice tone and to always keep others' feelings in mind. Doing so will show that we are genuinely nice people.

87

His Efforts

I must admit that there are times when I act rather childishly. When my husband apologizes, I'll sometimes stay mad instead of accepting his apology right away simply because I like the attention or because I want to stubbornly hold onto my anger.

However, I realized one day that such behavior was quite "un-nunlike," and that I should try not to do that anymore. My teacher encouraged us to recognize the efforts of others, no matter how small they may be. If James made the initiative to approach me, I shouldn't play games and turn him away. Most likely, it took a lot for him to muster up the courage to do that. I should listen to what he has to say and try to make an equal effort to mend things.

One night, we fought and I retreated downstairs. At one point, he came down to check on me and instead of letting that soften my heart, I held onto my unhappiness with stubborn resistance. It's true that the subject of our argument may have been upsetting and worthy of my anger, but upon reflection, I should have given him merit where there was. I should have accepted his gestures of kindness and encouraged them by responding in a positive manner. It would've been nice if I had acknowledged his efforts and had taken a step forward like he did.

Don't be like who I was. If he apologizes and you know it was very hard for him to do so, don't reject him. Instead, recognize his efforts and accept his apology with gladness. Let those little acts of goodness chip away at the force of your anger and be quick to forgive him when he tries. You will only encourage him to be better in the future.

88

Sunblock

One weekend, after a particularly tiring week slaving over our newborn baby, my husband and I finally had a babysitter for the afternoon. We were rushing to get ready so we could go out for the maximum amount of time. We were both tired and worn out but desperately needed a break. As I was getting ready, I grabbed a bottle of sunblock and impatiently found that the opening was clogged. I pressed down hard on the dispenser several times, trying to get the hole unstuck. Suddenly, a forceful stream of sunblock shot out of the opening and somehow squirted directly into my eye. I felt the liquid envelope my eyeball. My husband saw it too. I screamed and ran to the bathroom to wash it out. My eye was stinging like crazy. I wanted to cry. The week had been stressful already and now *this*, to top it all off.

When I came back out, my husband looked at me for a moment and then unexpectedly, he started laughing. He started laughing and laughing and laughing. I was confused at first but then really thought about it and imagined what the whole thing must've looked like to him. I had to admit, it was pretty ridiculous. At that point, I just let everything go and instead of crying, I started laughing with him. The two of us were just laughing on our bed thinking about how silly it was. When we were finally able to gather ourselves, my husband said to me, "At least your eye has sun protection now. You don't have to wear sunglasses."

Sure, some days can be long, tiring and stressful, but just laugh about silliness as much as possible. Don't hold on to things with such seriousness. Have a really good laugh once in a while and just release it all. Take things lightly. Laugh at yourself. Things can't always be perfect all the time. Life was not meant to be perfect. Allow yourself to be human and to see how humorous it all can be.

89

Brooms and Mops

was watching a real-life drama on T.V. once and was instantly captivated by the story. In it, an experienced teacher was about to teach a class full of wildly misbehaving students for the first time. This reminded me very much of my experience in Edu Park. She stepped foot into the classroom and was met by a scene of adolescent boys messing around in all corners of the room. No one had even noticed her walk in. The classroom was in complete disarray and I wondered to myself how this lady would begin teaching such a wild group. To my surprise, she started with something I was not expecting.

Instead of jumping straight into the rules and curriculum, she grabbed some brooms and cleaning supplies. Her first order of business was to clean the classroom. She organized the boys to sweep, mop and clean, which they were actually willing to do because it was something different and required physical exertion. Together, they tidied up their classroom until it was all neat and spotless. Only then, did the teacher start to conduct any type of class and the effects of the clean environment clearly reflected positively on the students. They were more calm, focused and ready to learn.

That day, I learned a very important lesson from watching her example. If you want success, you first have to make sure that your physical environment is neat and organized. Your surroundings are a direct reflection of your mental state. As a teacher, a clean classroom conveys structure, stability and security. When students walk into a neat classroom, they naturally feel safe, comfortable and at ease. It helps them behave better and become better students.

I have found that this concept applies in the home setting as well. Have you ever walked into a home that was cluttered, dirty and messy? Without knowing why, you were probably feeling uncomfortable and uneasy already. The residents of that space have already set themselves up for shortcomings at the subconscious level. Conversely, have you ever walked into an orderly home and felt completely at ease? Your spirit seemed to relax into the comfort of your surroundings and you felt safe. People naturally enjoy being in tidy places and it is also a show of discipline.

Therefore, as much as possible, try to maintain a neat environment. This will give you and your husband a pleasant place to come home to. It will make everyone feel relaxed and content. With a calm mind, the heart will be calmer and this simple step could prevent a lot of unforeseen troubles.

90

St. Rita

My husband and I got into a particularly bad fight once. We were in the car, driving home, and I was yelling. The baby was crying. When we got home, I was still so upset. I slammed the car door shut and instead of going into the house, I decided to walk around outside. I was furious.

Being alone outside in the cool night felt really good. I really needed some time by myself. When I reached the end of the neighborhood, some glistening Christmas lights from across the street caught my attention. They were from the Catholic church on the main road. Not ready to go home yet, I wandered over there under the comfort of dim streetlights. I find it lovely how the church doors are always open. It feels so welcoming and inviting. I walked across the open courtyard, surrounded by colorful lights, and sat on a bench. I had a perfect view of everything. The rain was falling lightly now. I stared at the colorful lights in front of me and an overwhelming thought flooded my mind. Those lights, although tiny in size, brought so much warmth in the dreadful darkness. Each tiny bulb lit up the atmosphere and inspired so much hope all around it. A voice suddenly seemed to speak to me: "In the same way, the smallest act of kindness can make a huge difference; its influence can run so far."

Surprised at the peace and wisdom I found in such a place, I started walking around. I came to the foot of a beautiful statue and read the inscription: St. Rita. I looked at this compassionate woman and tucked the name away into the back of my mind. I told myself I'd have to look her up one day.

Several weeks later, when my sister was visiting and I was standing over the playpen watching her play with my baby, I suddenly had a spontaneous urge to look up this St. Rita whom I had met at the church weeks before. Excusing myself, I commenced my impromptu research and was surprised at what I found. St. Rita was once a young girl who wished to become a nun. She encountered obstacles though and was forced to marry a cruel husband. He was not a religious man at all and her situation seemed hopeless. Miraculously, St. Rita was eventually able to transform her fearsome husband into a man of gentleness and faith. He used to beat her, as some stories go, but he ended up loving her to pieces and respecting her very much. For the last segment of her life, after her husband passed away, St. Rita finally fulfilled her wish of becoming a nun. Her story reminded me very much of my own, except I wouldn't go as far as to say that I have a cruel husband.

I couldn't believe there was a role model whose life mirrored mine so closely. Here was a girl who wanted to become a nun but got married instead and used her gifts in the realm of marriage. I had never come across another person who shared my life's ambitions. And yet, her statue was resting right across the street from my house almost overlooking my daily life. I found it all highly comforting and positively providential.

For the days that followed, I delved into her books. I was especially curious to know how she won over the love and admiration of her husband. The recurring themes I found in her practice were gentleness, patience, affection and peace. She didn't speak much and never preached her beliefs but lived out her religion through her actions. She always confronted harshness with gentleness and patiently waited for her husband to come around. Although she was denied her first wish of becoming a nun, she poured her love out onto all those around her and transformed so many lives.

St. Rita taught me that humility and obedience are the ways of the righteous and that such endearing traits can overcome any evil. I would like to encourage you to look further into her life story if it interests you. I hope that the path of this beloved saint will bring comfort to you during your dark times. May she act as a shining example of what one can achieve even in the midst of hopelessness and desolation. She has walked in our shoes before and shown us that *nothing is impossible.*

91

Another Angle

Nuns are very good at solving the problems in their lives because they are such contemplative beings. One thing I've learned from them is that if you get stuck in a bad situation, don't stay stuck. Don't give in easily and think that's just how you'll spend the rest of your life. Get moving, search your brain and find a path out. Maybe from the angle you're seeing things, there's no solution. The road is blocked. You might have to adjust your position ten degrees to the right to see a pathway, or you might have to dangle yourself completely upside down to get a different perspective. But whatever the case, don't succumb to the depression and the misery. Don't stay stuck in a bad situation. Get used to using your creativity to find a way out towards happiness. There is always a way out.

One day, a relative who lived nearby told me she was on her way to my house to pick up something for work and to visit my baby. Although I was usually happy to see her, hearing of her coming that day did not please me as I was experiencing mental burnout and wanted to be alone. I was filled with dread actually after she called me and thought I was stuck in a bad situation. From my angle, things didn't look good. The road was blocked. But after shifting my perspective a little bit, I suddenly realized that her visit meant she could help me babysit for a little while. I could use that time to run to the market which I really needed to do and it could actually become a sweet little break for me. I just needed to change the angle at which I was viewing things. That is just a small example of how being creative can lead to different positive outcomes. Sometimes, life throws us much bigger curveballs, but the idea is still the same.

When you're playing a video game and you drive off the road, you were not designed to stay off the road. You were designed to find a way to get back on the path in any way possible and to finish the course. It's the same in life. You were not meant to stay down in a tough situation. Get used to dusting yourself off and finding the path to happiness again. Don't give up until you truly feel content and finish the course with flying colors.

92

The Doormat

For the longest time, I thought loving someone meant letting them do whatever they wanted to me, even if I ended up being treated like a doormat. If I refused or turned someone away, I would be racked with guilt, feel as if I were displeasing them and being less of a spiritual person. But *finally*, after years and years and years, I learned that loving someone does not always mean fulfilling their every wish or tolerating everything they do. Sometimes, being loving means setting clear boundaries on what is acceptable and what is not. It may even entail fighting back and letting them know, "What you are doing is absolutely not okay." People will only treat you how you *allow* them to treat you. Even my spiritual teacher was known to be very strict whenever the time called for it.

When my older daughter turned two, the teachers at her daycare started transitioning her into a new class. All the other students in her new class were older than her and she got picked on. One day, a boy took her face and squeezed it really hard, somehow resulting in some scratches on her face. He also slammed a toilet seat really hard on one of her fingers. When I heard about it later, I was so heartbroken. I couldn't stand for that to happen to her.

When James' mom heard as well, she started coaching my daughter on what to say in order to defend herself. I thought she was so cool for doing that. Sometimes bullies need to be stood up to. And I wish someone had taught me that. I wish someone had taught me to defend myself, but no one ever did. Now, as a full-grown adult, I'm finally learning this lesson. It's okay to stand up to bullies. In fact, it's imperative. It's imperative to love yourself enough to stand up to them. Loving yourself means protecting your most basic rights and not letting others mistreat you. It's very simple. Sometimes, the love you wish for others is the love you need to give yourself.

In the past, I made the mistake of thinking that compassion equated to being a submissive doormat. But now I know that compassion and strictness can exist simultaneously. One good example I can think of to illustrate this dynamic is a mother and her child. Moms are full of compassion when it comes to their children. However, they are also strict and stern in order to teach them and to make sure they are brought up well. Letting kids do whatever they want spells disaster and is very unwise. It could ruin their lives forever. Therefore, harshness is sometimes necessary as an expression of kindness.

Now, whenever people are unfair to me, especially those who are close to me, I make it known that I am not okay with it. Being treated like a doormat is never acceptable. Tolerating oppressive behavior is not an act of love, it is a show of one's lack of self-worth. And if you really think about it, how can you truly love others if you don't even know how to love yourself properly? You can't give away what you don't have. Therefore, treating yourself well and making sure you are protected is essential.

93

The Lined Wastebasket

Thoughtfulness is heavily emphasized in religious life, but it's not always easy to know how to apply it to our daily actions. Thankfully, my husband is very thoughtful and has taught me a thing or two about it. If my husband takes my car out for a drive and sees that my gas is low, he will fill it up for me. There's not even a question about whether he'll do it or not. I know he will. That's just part of his character. When it's dinner time, he'll serve me first and make sure I'm taken care of before he serves himself. He's always thinking about how to make people's lives easier. He considers others in everything he does.

Throughout the years, I have tried to become more like him. I try to think one step ahead for those around me and to see what they may need in the future. I find that people really appreciate such gestures, even if they are small.

One time, my hands were full and I was trying to take out the trash in the bathroom. I pulled out the trash bag and saw that the waste basket had been pre-lined underneath already. Since my hands were full, I was grateful and surprised that I had one less thing to do. In that moment, I understood how nice those little thoughtful acts really are. They really make a difference. Then, I realized that I, myself, had pre-lined that waste basket weeks before. I had just forgotten. So in fact, I had been moved by my own thoughtfulness. I smiled to myself.

Being thoughtful is really a pleasant trait to implement around the house. When everyone is trying to do what they can to make others' lives easier, the atmosphere becomes so sweet.

94

In-Laws

My sister and I were sitting on the bleachers at an amusement park, waiting for a show to begin. The seats were filling up quickly under the hot sun. Suddenly, a video appeared on the big screen in front of the arena. In it, we saw our magnificent earth spinning majestically in space, then an array of different animals to represent distinct members of our families. For the little brother, they showed a lizard calling out obnoxiously with its facial flaps flared out. For the in-laws, they showed two rams forcefully ramming their horns into each other. Everyone in the audience laughed at the implication of this. It is well known that dealing with in-laws can be difficult, not unlike two rams making a head-on collision.

I must admit, dealing with in-laws can be tricky for many reasons. From what I've personally observed, in-laws can sometimes harbor sadness from parting with their children after marriage. Often, this leads to complicated feelings of bitterness or jealousy which can translate to unpleasant behavior. Or they may be worried about their child's well-being, thus putting extra pressure on the child's partner or becoming too involved in the relationship altogether. Whatever the case, it's a complicated business to merge families together and so, it comes as no surprise that dealing with in-laws can be messy.

Although I got along fairly well with my husband's mom (the main parent in his life), the real turning point that changed my feelings positively towards her occurred after I became a mom myself. Becoming a mom was very difficult for me. I was unaware of how grueling it would be to bring up a helpless newborn. I thought the hardest part of the process would be labor and physically getting the baby out itself. That's what everyone always stresses. But no, the real difficulty for me lay in the first several months of the baby's existence where I had to tend to her around the clock. The lack of sleep, often painful extraction of breast milk, exhaustion, and feelings of being overwhelmed sent me spiraling into depression the first couple weeks.

It was also at this time, however, that I developed an incredibly profound appreciation for all mothers out there. I felt bonded to all the women who had experienced what I was experiencing. I especially felt a deep gratitude to my own parents who had carefully raised me and sacrificed for me in this new way that I wasn't accustomed to. I couldn't imagine how they managed to raise my sister and me into full-grown adults. It seemed impossibly far away from where I was. I was completely humbled. This monumental thankfulness also extended to my mother-in-law as I recognized that she too, had put in her fair share of sweat and tears for my benefit. She had made many sacrifices herself to painstakingly raise the man I love from a tiny fetus to a man now standing over six feet tall. Without her nurturing hand, careful tending and loving heart, I would not have had my husband who has brought me so much happiness in life. Upon realizing this, my feelings toward her changed from simply ordinary to full-fledged thankfulness. I knew that I owed her everything.

No matter how terrible your in-laws seem to be, you always have this point of reflection to fall back on. When you remember that your spouse's parents raised your beloved best friend, when you realize that they did everything in their power to bring up the person you love most in the world, how can you harbor any ill will towards them? No matter what, this will forever be a reason for you to forgive their shortcomings. There is nothing that cannot be worked out with these people who have given you the best gift in life.

95

The Gifts in the Mess

We all desire a positive life with positive experiences. We resist the difficult and the ugly. But I've learned that even the most horrible experiences contain gifts. Everything that comes to us is meant to *serve* us. This was not always easy for me to see however. During the stage of my life when I was still acting as a doormat for others, I finally broke down one night from the unfairness of it all.

Crying in the shower, I asked into the air, "*Why?*" The words could barely come out, I was hurting so much. I kept asking why. "Haven't I been a good girl?" I breathed. I felt like I was being punished for all my kindness. My whole life flashed before me and I saw all the times when I had been mistreated by others. I wondered why I had been so cruelly trampled on so many times. But a few days later, I understood that I needed to go through all of that pain to realize that I had to stand up. I had to break free. No one could do it for me. I felt that the angels felt bad for my pain and it hurt them to watch. But even they couldn't fix my life for me. I had to stand up on my own. I had to launch myself into a new version of me, a stronger version of me that *needed* that pain in order to propel forward. It was all necessary for my growth.

Reflecting back on that time and seeing how strong and independent I've become, it all becomes clear to me. The bad situation was necessary for the birth of a new me. Therefore, even the horrible things that happen to us are gifts. Nothing happens by chance. Everything contains a blessing.

96

Starting First

It's easy to think that if we start something before another person, we'll always come out ahead, further and faster. We'll be much more advanced. But I've seen too often on the spiritual journey, that that isn't always the case. Just because someone starts on the virtuous path first doesn't mean they'll come out ahead in the end. Everyone is at a different level in terms of their spiritual growth. And some people who appear to have gone *far* off the course actually have seeds of greatness that are lying dormant on the inside of them. They only have to be spurred on to the spiritual path to excel far ahead, leaving everyone in amazement.

Therefore, even though you may be the one who starts learning the virtuous path first, don't be surprised if your spouse eventually surpasses you. Even though your spouse may appear to be lost in his ways or hopeless in changing, don't underestimate the greatness that can come bursting forth once he is on the right track. You don't know what's hidden on the inside and what he's capable of once the right conditions are present. He might just take off when he's exposed to new concepts and no one will have even seen it coming.

Often in my life, I have witnessed my husband go far beyond me. Although I've been pursuing the path of virtue for much longer than him, I have seen him surpass me in many ways. Naturally, he has a selfless heart that constantly thinks of others. Therefore, when he comes in contact with the teachings, he is able to put them into practice far better than me because he already has the predisposition for goodness. Contrary, I often feel that my personality tends towards selfishness so it takes me longer to learn things.

Another example is that my husband is naturally hard working. So once again, when he comes across the teachings, he is not lazy at applying himself. He puts in his whole heart and works tirelessly for the sake of that which he believes in. On the other hand, I am naturally lazy and like to take the easy way out so my learning is slower overall.

In the beginning, when we were dating, I was filled with self-pride and thought that I was better than him in terms of spirituality. He was still partying and drinking at the time. But now, I can see that he is far ahead of *me*, leaving me in the dust. He has gone on so far ahead that I have much to learn from *him*. He has clearly surpassed me in just a few short years. I have humbly learned that you should never judge someone for where they appear to be on the path at the moment. Looks can be deceiving. Give them a chance. Give them an opportunity to rise up and they may very well surprise you.

97

Reaching Out

Late one afternoon, I was taking out the trash to the community dumpster. A voice caught my attention and I saw that it was a little girl whom I had seen several times before in the neighborhood. She was waving at me sweetly from a distance and smiling. I was surprised at this because previous encounters with her had led me to believe that she was a rude little brat. I always ignored her when I saw her. But looking at her now, smiling at me like an angel under the warm sun, I felt moved that she looked so happy to see me. It left a rather pleasant impression and I happily waved back.

This encounter made me remember something a nun had mentioned to me before. *Why must we always wait for others to show kindness to us first before we are moved to feel something towards them? Compassion should be a very active force, not an idle one that stays holed up in one's corner. It should be a passionate and friendly energy that reaches out to others, showing warmth and care.* As an aspiring practitioner, I expected more from myself.

In my marriage, I thought about all those times I resented my husband for not saying or doing something I wanted; for not demonstrating love as I wished. "Why don't you care about me?" I would ask silently to myself. "Why don't you come talk to me? Love me?" But rarely had I asked, "What more can I do for you?" or "How do I show you I care?" My mentality had been so wrapped up around myself. But compassion is a sentiment that requires one to let go of selfish thinking and to ask, "How can *others'* pain be alleviated? Are they lonely or sad? How can others be happy?"

A compassionate person consumes themselves with all these questions and actively works to find solutions for them. They do not waste around, waiting endlessly for others to come to them. They throw themselves out there and do all that they can to make people's lives better.

That little girl opened my eyes to see how my focus had been all on myself and how being compassionate involves a different attitude altogether. As she stepped out to say hello to me, she demonstrated the energy that is present behind the true essence of kindness. She reminded me that being kind is not a passive undertaking, but requires action, effort and courage.

98

Healthy Mind

If you regularly tune in to the news, you may easily be bombarded by a lot of information that can be scary. My friends liked to circulate stories about scams and food dangers, all of which fueled my fear of a toxic world. I would insist to my husband that we had to make drastic changes around the house.

"Nothing but organic food from now on!" I would demand, among many other demands. My husband would always get annoyed and have something to say back, sparking arguments between us.

I realized over time that my fears and my worries were probably more toxic than the actual foods I was putting into my body. The stress I was causing those around me was also probably more harmful than anything else. Being around religious practitioners showed me that being happy is actually the strongest protection against disease. Filling your mind with positive thoughts is the best way to make your health flourish. It is my belief that the physical can be overcome by the mental.

Of course, it would be nice to be informed about the things that are harmful in life and what changes can be made. Being educated is always a good thing. But don't live your life in fear of everything. Don't push your family too far. Try your best and if you are not able to make certain changes, stay happy and remain positive. Think of all the things you are still grateful for.

For example, our family couldn't switch to organic produce completely. But instead of fixating on that, I changed my thought process. I started feeling grateful that I had plenty of food to eat. A lot of people go hungry in this world, many even starve. But I always have plates of warm food in front of me. There is nothing more fortunate than this. The positivity that filled my mind from receiving the food was perhaps more healing and nourishing than the actual food itself. Your thoughts are powerful things that can change the chemical make-up of your body. Use your mind to nurture yourself in the best ways possible. It is your greatest protection.

Remember, always keep a positive perspective. Don't fall into the trap of negative thinking. Your mind is more important than your physical body. It can overcome anything.

99

His Love

The fact that I wanted to become a nun might already tell you that I'm happy owning just a few material things. It makes me happy when I wear my shoes to the point where they have holes in them. It gives me a sense of accomplishment to know that I've put my shoes to great use and really maximized their full worth. Simplicity is my way. I enjoy having just a handful of things and don't like to waste resources. I recycle and bring cloth bags to the market. I always think twice about throwing something away, wondering if there can be another use for it. I try my hardest to put the smallest dent on the planet as possible.

My husband is the opposite of me. He is extravagant and enjoys being surrounded by things of luxury. He doesn't mind throwing stuff away by the truckload. Sometimes, he'll crush a plastic bottle in front of me and smile mischievously because he knows I can't recycle it anymore. His ways are not my ways. And his ways of loving me are not always my ways either. For example, one time, he went to a warehouse sale with a friend and bought me ten pairs of shoes. He dumped them all out on the floor in front of me and smiled sweetly. I was so shocked. I had never owned ten new pairs of shoes at once before.

Every year, he switches out my cell phone for a new one even though the one I have is always in perfect working order. My heart always breaks a little when he takes away my existing phone and when I think of all the unnecessary electronic waste I'm creating.

When we go out to eat, he orders so much food that the waiters often ask if more people are joining our party. James always smiles and says, "Nope, it's just us." He just wants us to sample everything and whatever we can't finish gets thrown away. "It's okay," he'll tell me. "Don't worry."

There were times during this process when I felt rather uncomfortable with his ways. I felt so wasteful and extravagant that it was hard to swallow. My minimalistic self often watched in disbelief as plates and plates of food went straight into the garbage. Sometimes, I wanted to get angry because I felt like he was being too careless.

But then one day, it occurred to me that that was just his way of loving me. He wants to spoil me with material goods and allow me to enjoy life in every way. That was how his mind processed things. Instead of focusing on all the waste and all the extravagance, I decided to focus on his *intention*. His intention was always to make me happy. He actually didn't have to spend all his hard-earned money buying me shoes or phones or decadent meals. But he did so because he felt it was worth it. He felt that providing his family with luxuries was worth the price of working hard. That was just how he demonstrated love.

When I realized this, I decided to just kick back and let him love me in his own way. Instead of lecturing him and picking fights about his habits, I learned to just accept and appreciate what he does for me. By doing so, I avoid hurting his feelings and allow him the happiness of knowing he did something nice for me. His ways are not my ways, but that's okay. His intentions are gold and really, that's all that matters.

100
The Closed Garage

One of the things I loved about moving into James' neighborhood was how open everyone seemed. Kids would always be playing outside. People would leave their garage doors open and wander in and out of the house at random. Our next-door neighbor often hung out in her garage, where she set up a table and chairs, and I would wave hello to her whenever passing by. She was a very trusting person who often let us into her house. She even kept her back door unlocked which just reflected the trust she had of the world.

One day, however, my husband came home and told me that our neighbor had been robbed. Someone had entered her house through the back door and ransacked her home while she was out front, gardening. My heart broke to hear that such a terrible thing happened to our sweet and open-hearted friend. From that day forth, I sadly watched her garage door close more on the neighborhood. The chances of catching her outside were less frequent and of course, she started keeping her back door closed as well.

From that instance, I learned that trust is a very fragile thing and once broken, the effects are nearly irreparable. It's very hard to fix something once it's broken. In the same way, it's very hard to trust again after a betrayal. The damage is always there and doesn't fully go away.

Afterwards, whenever I walked by that closed garage, my mind traced back to the one event which caused such an outcome to happen. A betrayal had occurred and the doors were now shut. It was a good reminder for me to take care of the trust given to me by those I love. For example, I never want to hurt my husband or do him a wrong when he has such faith in me. Otherwise, his door might be closed on me forever. I told myself that trust is a delicate thing and I must take care of that trust to my best ability. If I don't, it could ruin everything I've worked so hard for. It's much easier to manage the upkeep of trust than to glue the shattered pieces of something back together again. That is one lesson you don't want to learn the hard way. Be careful with others' faith in you. Protect their trust with your whole heart and don't let it break.

101

Fragile Sprout

If your spouse suffers from low self-esteem, the best way to build them up is to *praise* them. Constantly praise them. That's what my guru taught me. When they improve a little bit in one area, praise them abundantly and with sincerity. Keep in mind that any small improvement they made probably took a ton of effort. After all, every habit is so hard to change. Although the change they made may look really easy to us, it might have actually been extremely difficult for them. Everyone struggles in different areas. The more you acknowledge where they improved, the more of that behavior you will get.

During my time working with children in the boarding school, I found that a lot of them lacked self-confidence. They were like fragile little sprouts, standing vulnerably among the elements. If they received a lot of criticism, they would collapse and stop growing. But with attention and praise, they would get stronger to stand on their own and start flourishing. Words build them up and allow them to see their own strengths. As a teacher, I had to be extremely careful in tending to those little sprouts and to make sure they were protected.

Adults are often the same way. Those who lack confidence can benefit immensely from the encouragement and support of their loved ones. If your spouse could use a little picking up, be the one to cheer them on. Be their biggest fan and lift them up. Encourage their endeavors and show your full support for all that they do. If they have a dream or an idea that seems crazy to you, don't shoot them down right away. There are enough nay-sayers in the world. We don't need any more of those. We need more believers and positive influences.

If your spouse created a project that he wants your opinion on, try to see the effort that went behind it before delivering a judgement. Even if it doesn't look that great on the surface, it may have taken him countless hours. If you focus on the effort, then you will have more appreciation for what was done. Always see the good in things and be quick to praise. Build up those around you with positive words. Be encouraging, always. And be mindful of those fragile sprouts existing around you. They could really use your support.

102

Some Days Suck

Let's just face it. There will be times where you neither have the drive nor the motivation to be the bigger person or to fix the problem at hand. You may feel completely burnt out and drained, not wanting to exert any effort into making things better at all. And that's okay. That's absolutely okay. You are only human. We all are.

Allow yourself the freedom and space to know that you can't always act "nun-like." You fight the good fight most of the time and that's really good already. It's fine to take breaks and recharge those mental batteries when you need to. After all, we're in it for the long haul and have to rest for the journey ahead.

When I feel burned out, I like to channel my energy into something I enjoy, something that makes me happy. For example, I might go out into the garden and do some reading. It relaxes me so much. Or I might tidy up my closet because I've been meaning to do it for a while. I find that getting my body physically active is especially helpful in helping me feel better. It gets my mind thinking less and my body doing more. Also,

I make sure that I've had something to eat or that I've been properly rested. This is so important. Sometimes, taking care of my physical body is all it really takes to get me feeling good again.

But most importantly, I don't give myself too much pressure to bounce back right away. I just take as much time as I need to heal and re-center myself. Interestingly enough, the more I'm in this relaxed and happy state, the quicker peace and forgiveness come to mind. Before long, I'm able to gather myself again and enter the arena with a calm and stable demeanor.

Don't be afraid to give yourself space and time, even if you need *lots* of time. Just accept that some days, you'll want to get away from everything and that's fine. There's no rush to mend things, no rush to make things right; everything can wait. It's okay to step back for a moment. The journey of a lifetime requires it.

103

Together

There was a period of time after my first child was born when I felt like I was drowning in chores. Even though I didn't have to "work" and was able to stay home, I felt like I was barely able to finish everything that was required of me. I would work like a mad woman all the way up to the last second until my husband came home. It was like that every day and I often felt worn out.

One day, my husband surprised me by coming home one hour early from work. He helped me with my chores and it felt nice to have an extra set of hands. To my amazement, everything got finished in no time at all. Soon, we were relaxing on the couch together with lots of time to spare. I couldn't believe what a difference his presence made. It really allowed me to see how everything is easier with a partner. The difference was just too striking to ignore.

The nuns believe that doing things with others is always a better option. It makes everything easier and more successful. But so often in my marriage, the opposite seemed true to me. Many times, I thought, "Gee, everything would be easier if I just did things by myself." Then I wouldn't have to account for someone else's feelings or opinions. I wouldn't have to work out so many details with another person and smooth out so many differences. But through it all, I forgot the beauty of what it means to be part of a team. Marriage is designed to make life easier for two people. At the end of the day, two is more fortunate than one. You double the strength, double the help, double the thinking power, divide the burden and share the load. Things get accomplished on a bigger scale with less effort and more concentrated power.

Having my husband come home just one hour earlier from work did wonders in changing my perspective and allowed me to see that the nuns were right. It's true that sometimes differences need to be worked out between us. But that's not the end of the picture. When the drama and conflict is overcome, there is great beauty to be found. Being part of a team allows better things to come forward and I had not recognized that for so long. That day though, I understood what a blessing it is to have a companion in life, and I reminded myself to cherish the presence of my husband who actually makes so many things easier for me.

104

Snowy Mountains

It was raining really hard one particular week and I was stuck at home much of that time with my baby. I live in an area that's relatively sunny year-round, so a downpour of that magnitude was quite unusual. Day after day, the rain fell and our spirits seemed to wane with the never-ending storm. Grayness enveloped us as we wasted away indoors.

At the first sign of light, I packed my baby in the car and took her out for some fresh air. On the freeway, as I was coming out of a curve, the most gorgeous sight suddenly came into view and stunned me. I saw the whitest, purest, snowy mountains I had ever seen laying majestically before me. It was breathtakingly beautiful. I couldn't take my eyes off of this magnificent sight. As I continued driving and admiring the beauty of this amazing phenomenon, I couldn't help but think back on the dreadful storm that had produced it. The unusually long storm had given birth to a thing of such wonder. It reminded me of that saying I often heard people say: Rainbows always come after the rain. That phrase always seemed a bit clichéd to me. But that day, with the snowy mountains in front of me, I felt deeply in my being that good things really do come from harsh situations.

I started to reflect back on my life and how years ago, my deep and profound desire to become a nun was not granted. I went through a storm; a very long storm that lasted nearly ten years. But now, I have an opportunity to write a book and to share a message that's important to me with the world. This new journey is my snowy mountain; it is a beautiful thing that came only after a long season of pain. The thing I realized in my car that day is that there is always hope. No matter how bleak a situation appears to be, the horizon is bound to change sooner or later. It cannot rain forever. At some point, the sun must come out. Similarly, when a situation hits rock-bottom, there is nowhere left to go but up. The natural laws of our world are perfectly balanced in that way and do not allow for a thing to stick around for very long. So whatever tough situation you may be in, know that the storm will pass. And inevitably, something beautiful will be waiting for you just around the corner.

105

Nature's Healing

Religious practitioners are often found living and walking among nature for inspiration and it's not hard to see why. For myself, there's no experience more spiritual than perhaps being in the heart of a sacred forest. The smell of the moss and trees seem to purify me from within; the cool and hydrating mist feels so good against my skin. Being among the trees always makes me feel so peaceful and whole. I reckon I could spend an eternity just hiking through a forest and never get tired of it.

Growing up, I often felt physically weak and tired. However, I noticed that every time I came into contact with nature, I would seem to be given new energy; I seemed to grow stronger and healthier.

I realized just how powerful nature was when I was at my most stressed out time in life. At that point, I was in my mid-twenties and was teaching in a middle school. I had seven full classes of students and was swamped every day, responding to their journals. A lot of the students had begun relying on my journals as an outlet and as a source of relief from their hectic lives, something I had not foreseen happening. Feeling the weight of their tender emotions spilled on paper, I spent day and night writing paragraphs in response to their entries. With hundreds of journals stacked on my desk every day, there was no time for anything else. I would sit there for hours writing away feverishly, only to go to sleep and do it again the next day.

One day, in the midst of writing, I started feeling sick. Nausea started overtaking me. Despite the lack of time, I dropped my pen and went outside. I needed to get some air. On a whim, I picked up my bike and rode around the block for five minutes. I felt the fresh air enter my lungs and the sun warm my face. I took in the trees and the sky and felt the stress peel away from my body. Nature seemed to absorb all of my stale energy and breathe life into me again. Five minutes was all it took. That's when I realized how powerful nature is in healing and replenishing the spirit.

After this understanding, I would often encourage James to approach nature with me as well. He did not have the habit of doing so but I knew he could benefit from it immensely because he was often anxious and stressed out. Although he was reluctant to the experience at first, he began to enjoy being submerged in nature over time and would even suggest new hiking places for us to visit. I could sense the same peace that filled me up, filling him up. I could see the anxiety being lifted from him whenever we were out together, trekking through the great expanse. I'm thankful for what nature has done for us and I highly encourage you to spend more time outdoors with the one you love too. It will bring much relief and restoration to the both of you.

106

Transparent

I read a beautiful notion once about the spirit realm being free of any barriers. Whatever one spirit thinks is fully exposed to other spirits. Everyone is completely transparent and there is no divide. Some might actually find this to be scary and invasive of one's privacy. But in terms of a marriage, I think there is much beauty in being able to share all of your soul with someone. That is what I aspire to in my relationship. I want to completely bare my truest form and have absolutely nothing to hide from my partner.

Sometimes, when I'm lying in bed with my husband and we're huddled close together with our foreheads touching, the moment feels so *pure*. We're both so exposed to each other and have nothing to hide. He knows all of me and I know all of him. It's a bond of the deepest kind because we choose to remain open and vulnerable, withholding nothing. Those moments of innocence and purity seem to offer me a glimpse into heaven. I can only imagine that's how the angels are in their realm of transparency. My goal is to only remain more honest and true to the one I've chosen to share my life with; to strive for holiness so that in the end, I am unafraid of becoming truly visible.

107

French Class

During the summer before high school, I enrolled in my first foreign language class: French. My sister had taken French during high school and it seemed like a beautiful language to learn. What I wasn't prepared for was how disorienting and difficult it would be to adjust to another language. Right when we entered the classroom, the teacher started speaking in French and from that day forth, we were not allowed to speak another word of English.

Everyone was confused at first, but as the first couple of days passed, most of the students seemed to catch on. Sadly, I was not one of those students. I continued to struggle and no matter how hard I tried, I just didn't understand the new concepts presented to us. Paired with the fast-paced nature of the class, I became unbearably frustrated. Sitting in class one day, at the peak of my disappointment, I started to cry silently in my seat. It seemed like I would never learn French.

What I didn't understand was that learning a new language can be really hard and can require some time. Not everyone can adapt right away. Oftentimes, we have to grasp an entirely new way of seeing things without any points of reference from our previous experiences. We have to begin completely anew, which can be absolutely daunting. *But with time and practice*, it always gets better; it's always made easier.

That certainly proved to be the case for me in French class. After the first week had passed, everything suddenly clicked one day and I completely understood all the things we had been taught. It just took time for it to happen.

I bring this all up because learning to use virtue in the face of adversity can also feel like learning a new language; it could feel totally foreign.

It can be disorienting and uncomfortable in the beginning. "This hurts, this feels unnatural," one might think. "Should I really take the high road? It's too hard." But just like how muscles get built up with training, our mind of virtue can also be strengthened with repeated practice. We can become better and more fluent in virtue with time. Give yourself some space. Be patient. Although difficult, it is a worthwhile path to take because it leads us directly out of suffering. It is the one language that can completely alter the course of our lives in a beneficial way.

108

The Vision

If you come into our room, the first thing you'll see is a large, framed picture of us hanging on the wall. In it, my husband and I are looking happily at each other with our hands interlocked. We're standing on a wooden bridge, surrounded by trees in a park. It's one of my favorite pictures of us because we look happy together and the background feels so serene. I purposely asked my husband to hang that picture on the wall right in front of our door so that every time I walk into our room, I am reminded of the love I want in my life. It's an image that pushes me towards my goal of living harmoniously with my husband. I believe it's hard not to succeed when my surroundings are filled with positive reminders of success. Every day, I look at our happy smiles and carry that image into the rest of my day. It's made such a difference. If you have a happy picture that speaks to you and inspires you, place it somewhere where both you and your partner can see it. Let the image saturate your thoughts and naturally become your realities.

109

Inspiration

When I sense myself about to get angry or lose control, it helps to think of something that inspires me to be better. For example, recently, this source of inspiration has been my baby's face. When I reflect upon her innocence and purity, I am brought back to my center and feel moved to act in a better way. My heart is softened and I am also reminded of the innocence and purity that resides within me. She reminds me of all that I aspire to. At the same time, the image of her face tells me that I'm a mother now and I can't behave so childishly. For her sake, I have to be a model of maturity and respect. She will learn all of her habits from me so it is imperative that I pay mind to my actions.

After meditating on her image for a short while, I usually become more calm and stable, ready to proceed in a nicer manner. It always helps to be reminded of the good I want to be. It pulls me towards the light and helps me remain there. If you ever sense yourself about to get angry, I would like to invite you to do the same. Invoke an image of something that gives you strength just by thinking about it; something that lulls you to your better self. Meditate on this image and watch your anger effortlessly fade away.

110

The Diamond

We go to school to get an education. We become skilled in all the major subjects such as Math, Science, English and History. However, nowhere in our educational system do they teach the art of living a happy life. Students are not required to take classes on interpersonal relationship skills, how to live harmoniously with others or to live a life of quality. But those are the fundamental elements that make a person's life worthwhile.

Sure, becoming skilled in a subject-matter is important. But what use is that if one is direly unhappy, failing in all their relationships or unable to find meaning in life? I wish more was done to take care of the individual regarding their ways of living. There is nothing more important to life than being happy and living with purpose.

I guess that leaves it up to us to devise our own courses for our lives. We need to take full responsibility of our own well-being because if we don't, then who will? Set the bar high for your life. Constantly search for ways to rise above and tackle difficulties. Make yourself a rare species of human; a higher grade, shining brighter than the crowds like a diamond among pebbles.

With virtue as your guide, an extraordinary life is possible for you. You have the means to conquer any obstacle and you will not be so easily overcome by hardships. You will gather people to you as those with patient understanding are few in this world. You will naturally be respected and regarded as a person of higher class because of your self-discipline. Your life will improve in every way if you stick to the course of virtue. There are so few in the world who are dedicated to this mission, yet it is so vitally important to one's happiness. I hope you are one of those few. Press onward and make it your life's purpose to live a life of integrity and meaning. You owe it to yourself to live your best life.

111

Prayer Angels

One of the best things about being married to someone is you get to see sides to them that *no one else* gets to see—the sides that are most raw and real. It's a very special relationship that allows you into the inner world of that person. I know my husband shows a very tender side to me that I haven't seen him show anyone else. He trusts me and is able to reveal how he really is without fear of being judged or of not measuring up to societal standards.

I'm deeply grateful for being able to see my husband as he really is. It is a privilege to hold someone's trust. And with that gift, I'm able to do something for him that no one else is able to do either. I'm able to pray for him in the areas where I know he is weak. I know his shortcomings and where he needs help becoming better. So I secretly help him along by praying over those particular weaknesses.

For example, one of the areas he struggles with is overindulging when it comes to food. He loves rich and flavorful things. Over the years, it's wreaked havoc on his body and caused him to develop multiple illnesses. I pray over him that he'll be stronger to make wiser food choices to positively impact his health.

There are also other areas in his life that I help him pray over, in hopes that he can become a more whole and happy person. As his wife, I can pray for the things he needs the most because I have access into his most private self. I can act as his prayer angel and look closely after him, helping him gather strength for the difficulties in his path. I would like to urge you to be a prayer angel to your spouse as well. Take note of where they might need some help becoming better and quietly pray for them every day.

112

Beauty

Have you ever watched a show or a movie where a character had a nice-looking face? But, because they were the villain and started doing evil things, their face started getting uglier and uglier? They may have started out looking alright, but because their personality was ugly, it started showing on the outside.

I find that the opposite is true as well. Perhaps you've met someone in your life before that seemed "just normal" upon first glance. But with time, their inner beauty started shining through and you found them becoming prettier and prettier. A person's heart really adds to or takes away from their beauty in the long run. This is especially so in a marriage.

After you live with someone for a long time, you'll find their outer beauty less important and their inner beauty more important. After all, what use is a pretty face if the person is mean, unkind and constantly causing suffering? You'll find that the person, even if they seem to have a pleasant physical exterior, is no longer attractive in your eyes.

If one is always kind, thoughtful and loving, then they will naturally be adored, admired and loved. But if one is always selfish, negative and rude, then they are chipping away at their beauty and making themselves completely unattractive; no one will want to be around them no matter how pretty their face is. In the long run, beauty comes from the inside. Your heart is what is most important. If you have a beautiful heart and work at expanding your love, you will radiate with an inner type of beauty that others cannot ignore. Therefore, work at making your inner-self attractive. That is the way to lasting beauty that defies all physical laws.

113

Wine

If you come to my house, you will see a magnet on our fridge that says: We ought to be opening a bottle of wine! I'm pretty sure my spiritual teacher would not condone the consumption of alcohol, but when I saw that magnet, I just really liked the energy I felt behind those words.

To me, it's a reminder that if my husband and I are ever fighting, we should stop wasting time arguing and instead, we should be opening a bottle of wine. A bottle of wine signifies happiness, fun and celebration. I want to celebrate life more and fight less. I want to make the moment light and filled with laughter instead of hiding away in our separate corners filled with despair. When negativity wants to creep in, let's consciously shut it down and bring out the joy. Let's make the house ring with celebration whenever we can. Remember, we always have a choice and we ought to be choosing happiness!

114

The One Rule

We've gone over a lot of different concepts in this book and it may feel quite overwhelming to take it all in. "How do I remember everything?" you might ask. But it's actually quite simple. If you can just remember one rule, then you'll be set.

For every situation you encounter, remember to simply *act with love*. And that's it. Remember to act with love. Check your intentions to see if you're coming from a place of loving concern. Try your best to make every decision out of kindness and with the other person's well-being in mind.

No marriage is perfect, so you don't have to give yourself too much pressure about that. Nothing on earth was intended to be absolutely perfect. But you succeed when you choose love above all else and then follow love's lead. Let love guide you in all of your ways. You can't go wrong when you make that the mantra of your life.

Sometimes we may appear to do something nice for others, but actually our motivation is fueled by selfishness or deceit. If possible, be wary of such motivations and try to act according to your highest good. Watch your heart like a thief and nip those bad intentions in the bud; they only result in suffering. On the contrary, when you wish others to be happy and act according to that wish, blessings always seem to follow. It is the root of all good things.

In the end, if you are ever in doubt on how to proceed during a tough situation, the answer is very simple. Check your heart; search it, and move forward in the most loving way possible. You cannot go wrong with love as your guide.

115

The Temple

I thought my life was over when I didn't become a nun. That was what I had built my whole life around. But years later, I realized that my thinking was too rigid during that time. I felt I could only be a nun in the physical sense for it to "truly count." I could only do monumental things in the center of holiness. But actually, being a nun is a *state of mind*. I can choose to have a pure and peaceful heart no matter where I am.

Recently, it actually occurred to me that my home is like a little temple with my husband being my co-practitioner and our children being little novices in training. We divide all the chores in the house and work to maintain peace under one roof. We overcome obstacles together and try to use wisdom to make big decisions. We grow together and advance together.

As for myself, I constantly have to be mindful of my actions and to be careful in choosing kindness over malice towards my husband. I have to watch my heart carefully and constantly evaluate my intentions. Every day, I am training in my own battlefield and exercising strength as a virtuous soldier. How is this any different than living in a temple?

I am very happy at coming to this conclusion. I feel so at peace with it. My path as a nun was not closed off. It was simply moved to another realm; a realm I never would have associated with nun-hood before.

But now, with my new understanding, I'd like to tell you this. If nuns were wives, they would *flourish*. They would give so much love and work at building so much peace. They would spread warmth and gentleness to all who surround them and allow sweet kindness into their homes. Surprisingly, they would be laid back and easy-going because of their understanding natures. They would be tireless in making the world better no matter where they are because they are faithful servants of humanity. Simply put, they would be revered and adored by all. If nuns were wives, they would be jewels in the world, shining radiantly and brilliantly in the darkness.

As you step foot into your house, remember to always arm yourself with the right mentality. Tell yourself: "Now, it's time for raw practice. My home is my temple. It's time to put the most profound wisdom and illuminating compassion to use. Let me relinquish the evil within me and finally gain control of my own freedom. Let me love those in my life with an otherworldly kind of love and to make this house a warm beacon of hope." With this attitude, every circumstance can only build you up and make you stronger. You cannot go wrong. Any place can be your temple. It all depends on your heart.

To close, it is my greatest hope that this book brings out the inner nun in you. May your life become truly happy, meaningful and weightless in peace.

Sincerely,

Shani

ABOUT THE AUTHOR

Shani Chen is a formerly aspiring nun who is now married. She spent nearly two decades familiarizing herself with the philosophies of the nuns and their way of life. She enjoys pushing the boundaries, learning through life's playground and working with children. Her interests include teaching, music, and animals. She and her husband, who have been together for twelve years, enjoy their residence in sunny California along with their two children.

ACKNOWLEDGEMENTS

First and foremost, I'd like to thank my mom and dad. Thank you for always supporting the dreams of my heart, including this one! I love you both.

Thanks Su for all your help. I'm grateful to have you as a sister.

To Ellen, Roger and Cat—my extended family.

My little babies, your innocence and purity constantly inspire me.

Marilyn, I'm grateful for your words of guidance which have stuck with me throughout this entire process.

Thank you, Joanne, for all your encouragement when this book was only an idea.

Kris Carlson, your kindness and support has truly meant the world to me.

To Miss Black, who awarded me a trophy for writing when I was in fourth grade. Thank you for believing in me even when I was just a kid.

Special thanks to the Morgan James team who had faith in this book and made it a reality.

And lastly, to James, my soulmate. Thank you for taking me on this journey. I'm so honored to live my life with you and to call you my husband. You just don't know how much I love you.

I'D LOVE TO HEAR FROM YOU!

If you have any comments, questions or would like to tell me how you are living life as a married nun, please write to me at:

Shani Chen

P.O. Box 5617

Diamond Bar, CA 91765

Morgan James
Speakers Group

www.TheMorganJamesSpeakersGroup.com

We connect Morgan James published
authors with live and online events
and audiences whom will benefit
from their expertise.